I'm not a large,
I am a medium!

*Heartfelt memories of a lifetime
of mediumship*

ROY MACKAY
with
CORNELIUS CAVENDISH

BALBOA.
PRESS

A DIVISION OF HAY HOUSE

Balboa Press books may be ordered through booksellers or by contacting:

Balboa Press
A Division of Hay House
1663 Liberty Drive
Bloomington, IN 47403
www.balboapress.com
1 (877) 407-4847

Print information available on the last page.

Interior Image Credit: Sara Allison

ISBN: 978-1-9822-3375-4 (sc)
ISBN: 978-1-9822-3377-8 (hc)
ISBN: 978-1-9822-3376-1 (e)

Library of Congress Control Number: 2019912539

Balboa Press rev. date: 09/18/2019

Contents

Acknowledgements

It is with great gratitude that I acknowledge some of the many souls that I have met on my pathway in life.

I have had the privilege to have worked with some wonderful mentors, teachers and colleagues. I begin with the closest to me in life, my mother Thurza Doreen Mackay who moulded me as a child and whose strength was amazing. After my father Roy died, her role doubled to take on the roles of both parents for me and my five siblings. My mother is responsible along with my grandmother for my inimitable belief in the world of Spirit. Through my mother my father's spirit was always there guiding and protecting us.

I would also like to give thanks to my grandmother Alma Carter, a medium in her own right, whose spirit continues to mentor me to this very day.

My thanks also go to some more lovely people who have helped me in different ways:

To those in my early days of learning the spiritual journey: the dedicated mediums Margaret Macleese, Gloria and Madge all of whom encouraged and believed in me.

To Grey Wolf my spirit guide and the wonderful spirit inspirers who have worked tirelessly to bring me to the level of mediumship I possess now. Grey Wolf was, and is, a wonderful mentor, guide and bodyguard. He gave me the motto, "In search of excellence."

To Julie Williams, whose trusted assistance, wisdom, comradeship and support during spirit rescues has been invaluable, and continues to be so today.

To those whose stories are shared in this book, including those whose names have been changed to protect their confidentiality...thank you.

To Lisa Ley and family who have contributed information to this book and for the wonderful way they welcomed me into their home. Many thanks.

To Glen Kilburn whose spirit connected with me as we journeyed past the place where he transitioned to the next world, and to Barbara Kilburn and family for allowing me to share his story.

To Bev Doucette whose great support and tireless energy and ingenuity helped to create my first ever presentation in Canada.

To Sara Allison, the artist who provided the brilliant illustrations for Spirit rescue with awesome accuracy.

And to the wonderful friends I have met on this spiritual journey.

I would very much like to acknowledge my dear friend Cornelius Cavendish, who as an established author helped me so much. His expert knowledge and patience helped me to transform and expand my manuscript into the well organised and sometimes humorous account of my spiritual journey as a medium.

His wealth of knowledge on the subject and his eye for detail seemed never ending. Thank you so much Cornelius.

I have no hesitation in recommending Cornelius to all who wish to embark on their own road to publishing.

A profile follows on the next page

About Cornelius Cavendish

Cornelius Cavendish is a Sunday Times and Guardian reviewed author, with more than 40 years experience as a journalist and editor on subjects such as business, entrepreneurship, science and design. He has written, edited and ghosted articles for several international publications, mostly on finance or business. He is also a speaker and lecturer principally on: the art of writing and speaking; English Baroque architecture; the ancient civilisations of Iraq discovered by his great-grandfather, Hormuzd Rassam, at the dawn of Middle Eastern archaeology in the 19th century. He has a deep interest in the mind/body/spirit field, especially healing and house healing.

Cornelius's websites are:
www.crcwritingservices.com
email: cornelius@crcwritingservices. com

www.refreshingthespirit.co.uk
email: cornelius@refreshingthespirit.co.uk

Introduction

During my 45 years as a medium, I have had so many different experiences and met a huge number of people, and along the way I have frequently been asked questions about life after death, the Spirit world, what it is like to be a medium etc. So I have written this to share with you what I have found in the course of my mediumship and what I have learnt during all those years.

I will take you behind-the-scenes as it were, to show you what it means to be a medium and explain the many different ways in which the world of Spirit connects with us. I think you'll be both heartened and surprised by the stories I have to tell you. Some of the events I describe surprised *me* at the time. A few are chilling but with happy endings, and most will make you smile or even laugh. In my work as a medium I have experienced the whole gamut of emotions, not just mine but those of others, and all that I'm sharing with you here.

You will learn that the world beyond this one is very real, and that this other world is nearer to you then you may think. Our friends and loved ones who have departed this world are around us, and we can connect with them if we want to. They are just a thought away helping us with the challenges that we face. It was an epiphany for me when early on in my work as a medium I realised that those we have lost from our Earthly lives make every effort to help us in our world. When you need them the most they are with you.

Writing this book has brought back so many happy memories, and as you read this I hope you will feel some of the joy and wonder that I have felt. The title of this book came to me when I remembered a visit I made to a clothes store in Canada some years ago with my new friend Beverly. At one point she found a nice jacket for me and said: "That's a large." And I replied: "I'm a not a large I'm a medium." And we laughed. So join with me now as I take you on a journey of discovery.

Chapter 1

A Happy Start

If you had said to me as a teenager that one day I would be a medium I'd have said, "You must be joking, I'm going to join the navy." If you had then said, "In fact you'll be a medium by the time you are 21," I'd have said, "Come off it, no way." And yet, that's exactly what happened. I didn't become a *full-time medium* at that age, but I *was* a practising medium performing in Spiritualist churches in my early 20s.

It's been an amazing journey, and I'm so grateful for the experiences I've had and the opportunity to be of service. Now I'm looking forward to experiences yet to come knowing that they are on my pathway for a reason. I'm very passionate about the work that I perform, and I know that each day I'm still learning as indeed we all are. We are all being guided by spirit guides, angels and loved ones that have gone to the spirit world before us.

As you read about some of the trials and tribulations of myself and others, it is my hope that these experiences will resonate with your own personal history. More than that, I hope that my story will make you smile and even uplift you as you read of the messages that have been passed on from the spiritual realm giving proof of life everlasting. It is also my hope that you will realise we are all psychic, whether we choose to use our 'gift' or not.

Of course there was a time when even to talk of such things would have aroused suspicion, fear, threats or worse. Only a few hundred years ago this book would have been treated as evidence that I was a witch or sorcerer. Even if I had been seen as a healer who merely wanted to help the sick and for no financial gain, I would have been liable to hanging, burning or the infamous 'ducking stool', where if you drowned you were deemed innocent and if you survived you were deemed guilty and subjected to more atrocities. Fortunately we are in a different age, but even today in Britain when a public demonstration of mediumship is held the organisers are required to state that the demonstration is 'for entertainment purposes only.'

I've been giving public demonstrations for more than 40 years, but even now my legs still shake with every presentation, knowing that a large number of people are listening to my every word and hoping that they will get a 'connection' of their own that night. My heart pounds as I aim to give everything to make the evening touch people and see them connect with 'a tear or a smile.' When I've done that then I know that I've done my job as a practising medium and channel.

Early Memories

Looking back, perhaps it shouldn't have been a surprise that I became medium, because as a child I was brought up with Spiritualism and healing. My mother was a Spiritualist and my grandma was a medium and healer. There were many times when I would have an asthma attack in the middle of the night and my grandma who lived a few hundred yards away would be sent for to give me healing. One of my sisters recalled hearing a deep Zulu voice guiding Grandma when she gave me healing. I remember hearing a very powerful healing voice as I struggled for breath. Once the healing was over I would fall soundly asleep.

There were six of us children: four older sisters, Jacqueline, Carol, Linda and Sandra, my younger brother Bob and me. We grew up in a house just around the corner from where I live now in West Molesey near Hampton Court. Mum and Dad met during the Second World War. Dad was a Canadian from New Brunswick who had been sent over with his squadron at a time when the government thought that Hitler might invade Britain. He was stationed at Bushy Park not far from West Molesey.

Mum and Dad were a perfect match for each other, and they're both still warmly remembered in my neighbourhood today. They were always doing things for other people. In those days, it was open house in our neighbourhood as it was in many other places then. You were there for other people. For example, our neighbours would come round with their motorbikes and ask Dad to fix them, which he gladly did.

Many mediums say that they remember having psychic gifts at a very young age —sometimes even at the age of two. I'm not sure I remember anything at the age of two and I'm a little sceptical of people who claim to have clear memories of visits by spirits at such an early age. For me there were no magical tell-tale signs, and to be honest I don't really remember very much before my father died when I was five.

Losing My Dad

I can remember the day my father died it as if it were yesterday. It was morning and we were getting ready for school. Then unexpectedly there was a knock on the door. In our house, and probably in yours, when there was a visitor at the door it seems as if the whole family came down to be there. This day was no different. I still remember the tall man in a raincoat with jet black hair standing back from the steps. He spoke to Mum, "You may want to send your kids out; I have some bad news." So we were ushered upstairs to our bedrooms. One bedroom window was directly above the front door, and being the nosy one, I opened the window and hung out, just in time to hear him say, "I'm sorry I have to tell you, your husband has had an accident in Beauchamp Road and is dead." Yes, that is how bluntly I remember it and I remember the doctor coming too, and after that everything is a blank. Dad was only 38. He'd had a coronary. I sometimes think that if that had happened today with all that we know about CPR that Dad would still be alive.

Dad was a millwright and worked for a local firm near Tolworth. He was always into mechanical things and was good at sorting out mechanical problems. He owned a motorbike and a car. I think we were the first house in the street to have a car, a shiny Ford Popular. He used to start his old car up in the morning, and then he would let us sit in his car as long as we didn't touch anything while he was having his breakfast. We used to just sit there. As I think about it the smells of the leather and everything else in there just come back to me.

His motorcycle and sidecar, were very special to him. He'd tell us not to touch anything but of course we did. It was quite a big, powerful motorcycle. We used to try and push down the kick-starter to start it up, but because it was so powerful, I couldn't do it on my own. So my brother used to step on my foot and we'd try to do it together. The only problem was that one day it did actually kick back and we ended up flying through the air onto the lawn. When Dad asked what had happened we said we didn't know, and we hadn't touched it.

So many people remember my dad. Some years ago I was in our local working men's club one night with my wife and two kids, and my wife said, "There's a lady over there who keeps looking at you."

She just seemed to be staring at me. When the music stopped she came over to me held my face in her hands, and kissed me on the forehead and said, "I knew your Dad, he was a lovely man." Wow, that really touched me.

I've been told I'm like him in many ways. My mum certainly thought so, and my sisters have a funny story to prove it. Mum wanted to buy a new TV set and asked my sisters if they would come with her and then carry the TV into the house. But my sisters said why not ask Roy. So off we went to the TV shop. While she was discussing the TV she was going to buy I went to the salesman and asked him if the TV had a remote control. "Yes it has," he said.

So I asked him, "Does it come with batteries."

He said, "No, it doesn't, you have to buy them separately."

So I said, "Surely you can give her a few batteries when she is buying a whole TV set. He said, "Oh alright." Then he said, "That will all be £250."

So I said, "Is that the best price you can do.?"

Mum came over and said, "Roy do you mind? You're embarrassing me. *I'm* dealing with this."

"OK Mum," I said, and then turned to the salesman again and asked, "Is this the cash price?"

He said, "Well, I could come down."

But Mum came over and said, "No, I'm paying the full price."

We took the TV home and then after I'd gone my sisters came round to look. Mum said, "I'm never going shopping with Roy again — he haggled and haggled."

But my sisters said, "But Mum that's good, he wanted to get you a better deal."

And Mum said, "He's just like his father." I think that was one of the biggest compliments she could ever have paid me.

Mum worked hard to bring up six children all on her own. She worked as a cleaner and had three jobs. She would clean one school in the morning, then pick us up from school, then clean another school in the early evening, and then after our evening meal she would go off to a nightclub where she would do the washing-up and other bits of cleaning. So she was always working.

There was even a time when she worked in an orphanage and we used to have to go with her. Since there were children there we could stay with the children while Mum went off to do her work. I remember that orphanage well — it is where my hatred of cheese comes from. The orphanage was run by nuns who made a cheese sauce to go with marrow, and I told them I couldn't eat it because I was feeling sick and they said, "You'll sit there until you have eaten it and then you can play with the kids". It was shortly afterwards that Mum found out about that and decided that she didn't want to be part of that place. We never went back.

Everyone remembers my Mum. They will say what a hard-working lady she was, and what a strong lady she was to bring up all those kids on her own. Mum never wanted anyone else in her life, and she used to say the day your Dad comes and gets me I'm off.

Unlike many children I loved going to school and all

my schools were within walking distance of our house. I think what I loved was the environment; I liked being around people and learning about different people and that included learning about the teachers. We had a teacher called Mr Bacon and everybody used to say, 'I don't want to be in Mr Bacon's class.' Well, I ended up in Mr Bacon's class and we got on like a house on fire. He used to play gramophone records on Friday afternoons, and he would say, "if you behave we will have some music this afternoon."

There was a lot about school that I liked. I always did quite well academically and I was always placed in one of the top classes. Of course sometimes I was naughty. Our house backed onto the Senior School's garden, so if I was late in the morning all I had to do was just jump over the back fence and I was in the school grounds. So as far as I was concerned I had arrived in school on time. I knew the garden very well because I used to work in the garden which I loved. The teachers used to get me out of lessons to do jobs in the garden.

I think the only time I got into trouble was quite funny. We used to do cross-country running, and to start the run we used to have to go past my house. So at first my friends and I would just go ahead and do the runs, but after a while we found that there was never anyone at home at that time. I had a key, so instead of going on the run we went into the house and had a cup of tea. Then when the boys came running back past the house we would join them at the end. But on one occasion it had been a really rainy, mucky week so everyone had to run through streams and muddy ground, and we joined them at the end as we always did. When we went through the gate into school the Sports Master asked us if we had enjoyed the run, so I pretended to be out of breath with my asthma, and then he promptly gave us a clip round the ear, and said, "How come everyone else is covered in mud and you and you have your pristine white shorts on?" We even tried to say that we went the wrong way, but he wasn't having any of it.

We kept that a secret from our family until about two years ago. My brother-in-law was talking to one of the boys I went to school with, and he said, "We used to go in the house on the school runs and have tea with Roy!"

I don't remember a lot about our holidays. I know if Mum had the money we would go somewhere, I remember going to Clacton once. I think most holidays were a day out here and a day out there, because that was all we could afford. That was quite hard because when we were at home for the hot summer holidays you would go around to one of your friends, and they would say, "We're just packing and going away on holiday." It did hurt a bit that everyone was going on holiday and we weren't, but my fallback was always fishing.

I'd pick up my gear and go down to the river and fish, and I was quite happy doing that day after day. I would do that until it was dark. Mum used to say, "Be home before dark." And when it did start to get dark I would think 'one more fish, just one more fish,' but the minute I heard my sister calling my name, bearing in mind we were only 100 yards from the river (the river Mole) I knew I was in trouble, because that meant she had been sent out to look for me. But even when she turned up I would still say, "I just want one more fish."

So fishing was a big part of my life and my friends' life. If I could fish with my friends we would go together, but if not I would go on my own. I would dig up some worms in the garden, I couldn't afford to go out and buy bait, and off I went. I would sit next to the 'proper' fishermen, and I would watch them and take any tips from them. They would say, "You won't catch much with those little worms, we'll give you some," and then I would be happy as a sandboy just sitting there fishing. My dad used to fish in Canada. I like to think I got that from him.

Dad's obviously "still here," ha, ha

Although Dad had gone from this world physically there were many times when we felt his presence. We would have "little incidents" or "messages from Dad" as Mum used to say. I remember we had a lilac bush and roses in the garden, and we would often make up bouquets to take to the teachers in the primary and junior schools. We were told not to bring lilac into the house as Dad said it was bad luck. However, one day when Mum was a little 'low' we picked some flowers from the garden and wrapped them in newspaper for that professional look! I guess Mum made allowances for the lilac as she quite happily took them and put them into a vase, proudly displaying them on top of the TV. In those days TV sets were big, chunky, heavy objects with a wide flat top on which you could put things like vases and flower pots.

We sat watching the television that evening; in full view of the family, several flowers were lifted out of the vase one by one and dropped promptly onto the carpet. Only the lilacs had been taken out. Mum retorted quite calmly, "That's your dad. I told you he didn't like lilac in the house." There were many other small incidences of doors opening on their own and I remember a tap on the door many times.

At night time Mum would always take a glass of water to her bedroom and every night she would hear the glass 'ping' twice. I could heard this from my adjacent bedroom. Mum would say, "it's just Dad saying goodnight".

As life moved on for me, there weren't too many other spirit episodes. I did have visits from spirit people sitting on my bed, but there were no conversations, just visits. In my teens, these petered out as I discovered girls and motorbikes.

My Near Death Experience

In my teens I had a near death experience. It was when I was about thirteen and my mother had just given me my father's signet ring, saying that he would wish I should have it to remember him by. I was totally over the moon. I remember Mum saying to me, "Keep it safe", which I pledged to do. I often used to take it out of its hiding place and try it on my finger on numerous occasions and then return it safely after it had cheered me up somewhat.

Then at some point I felt it was time to place it on my finger and give it a showing. This was fine until the day came that some friends and I decided to go swimming at the local pool at Hampton Court after school. I decided to wear Dad's ring, and I was sure that it was firmly snug on my finger and I was confident that it would be fine there.

In the changing room there were several thoughts of removing the ring and locking it away with my clothes for safe keeping, but being me my intelligence was missing that day as I raced to join my friends in the pool. Displaying my dad's ring on my far from grown up finger I was off for some fun.

Countless times I jumped off the diving boards and fought and splashed with my friends in the deep end of the pool, and countless times I checked that the ring was safely on my person. I must have become too familiar with all this repeated checking because the time came when I looked and saw that it was gone. I felt like crying, my heart was pounding as I retraced my movements in the pool. I recalled that I had been swimming underwater testing my breath-holding capabilities. I was oblivious to any noise except from the beating of my heart. Again and again I swam down to the depths of the pool frantic in my search for my father's ring and again and again I came to the surface gasping for air fruitless from my search.

I took another deep breath and swam down with my belly touching the floor of the pool, my hands were scouring, hoping and praying to connect with the ring. I approached a small grill in the floor and placed my fingers in the holes with the intention of lifting it to check the channel below. The grill did not move so I attempted to secure a firmer grip. By now I was expelling a little air as my lungs were aching.

I realised I would need to surface and was trying to release my grip on the grill, but I could not get my finger joint free of the grill, and again my heart started to race as I pulled again as hard as I could. I could not free myself and I had expelled all the remaining air in my body as I tried once more for a release. I still remember the feeling of wanting to draw in air. I would have sworn that someone could see me below the water, but obviously they were too busy having fun.

I remember a remarkable peace came over me, the fear seemed to have left me. I felt very unusual, all sound had left my ears. I thought I was giving up when all of a sudden I hit the air at the top of the pool and my body gave out a gasp for air that I have never felt since that day. Somehow my finger had freed and I was 'taken' to the pool surface, but it was instantaneous; I do not remember ascending, only reaching the surface.

I left the pool as soon as I could lift myself out. As I sat on the side of the pool just wanting to cry I was aware that the noise of the other bathers had returned. Where had I been in those few moments that for sure had saved me from drowning? I had not seen the tunnel that others had seen or the light shining through from the far end. My life had not flashed through my mind. Somebody had placed me in, shall we say, a 'bubble' of protection, and wherever I was for those few seconds between life and death I did not need to breathe and I had no fear. Thank God for those moments that kept me from my last moments on this Earth. That was my near death experience and I wonder how many reading this can relate to those moments.

Going To Sea

When I was 13 and 14 I began to think about what I wanted to do after I left school.

I had my eyes on the Royal Navy. I was always sending off for information about *What you can do in the Royal Navy* and what you can learn, and I was really into that. That went on for a couple of years.

Just before I left school I took some entrance tests for the Royal Navy, got through my exams and had an interview and then later had a medical examination. I had a full medical and I was told it all looked good. I was then asked if I had had any particular health issues which were all on a list. One of these was asthma. So I said that I had had asthma but it was wearing off. I said I hadn't had an attack for a couple of years.

The doctor then asked, "Have you had any other symptoms such as colds?"

"Yes."

"In the last two years?"

"Yes."

"Are you sure it is not longer than the last two years?"

"Yes."

I couldn't understand why he asked the question in that way.

At the end he said, "If you had said to me that you hadn't

had a problem with asthma for the last two and a half years or 26 months, you would have been outside the limit that we set, and it would not have been a problem. But because you said you had had symptoms in the last two years that means that I have to fail you on the medical." So it was not going to be the Royal Navy for me.

Someone then said, "Why don't you try for the Merchant Navy, because any ship that is not in the Royal Navy has to have a crew." So my friend and I did 12 weeks training at Gravesend. For some reason my friend's training finished earlier than mine so he joined a ship before I did, but we did meet up eventually on a cruise liner, which I'll come to in a minute.

The first ship I ever went on was an oil tanker, the Esso Lincoln. I wasn't impressed with it. All the crew wanted to do was drink and gamble and smoke. But I wasn't on board all that long as I had an accident on board ship and had to be flown home. I had been working in the catering area serving the captain and some of the officers in a separate dining area. I would prepare some food for them and take it from the galley and make sure that they got their meals on time. That was my job. One day a skipper said to me, "I fancy some chips." There was a big fryer in the kitchen, and I had to use a metal baine marie and half fill it with boiling hot flat.

As I walked away from the kitchen I slipped on some sponge mixture that one of the other chefs had spilt on the floor, and in very slow motion, the metal container went up in the air and all the oil came down on one of my hands which blew up in seconds. My hand doubled in size. I was taken to the ship's doctor, who said, "You will have to go ashore at Hamburg." When I was there they said, "You can stay with us in hospital for four weeks and go back to the ship, or we can bandage everything up and send you back home, where the British doctors can do what they need to do." So I went home. Then I managed to get onto cruise liners which was lovely. That was a doddle.

I saw a lot of the world on the cruise liners, and then again something happened that resulted in my being flown home. I was on the SS Oronsay. Before we got into Canadian waters, people on the ship got ill with typhoid. Pigeons had got into the water tanks and human faeces had even been found in them. I didn't get typhoid, but sometime after typhoid has been discovered I had to go to the ship's doctor because I had a hangover after having had a few beers the night before. I was feeling groggy and sick, so I went to the doctor for a pick-me-up. He said he would have to carry out a full examination, and then at the end he said that with all my symptoms he would have to send me ashore. Even though I said I just had a hangover he said that he would have to do that. So I went into hospital in Vancouver Bay for a few weeks, and then the ship moved on, so again I was sent home.

So as you see I don't do things by half in my life!

Then I had a couple of weeks break. I tried to contact the friend I was at school with, and I found out that he was on a ship called the SS Chusan. I went to the P&O office in London, and it said the SS Chusan needed one person. So the next time the ship came in for a refit I joined as a bell boy to the stewards which is what my friend was. He and I had great fun. There were lots of girls and lots of fun and we got chased off in places where we shouldn't have been.

We did loads of Mediterranean and Caribbean cruises. These would last only about four or five days at a time. We went all round the Mediterranean, Croatia, Slovenia (then part of Yugoslavia), Greece, Turkey. We spent a year or so together on these cruises, and then we decided to come home and have a holiday. And we just never went back. It was never a full-time job anyway. I'm not sure what we did next. I think we got jobs gardening.

So all that seafaring only lasted two years. That is me. I don't seem to stay with anything very long. One of my quotes is that when I say that I have been a medium for 45 years I can imagine my mum saying, "You couldn't do something for 45 minutes, your attention goes on to something else."

Some time after I came back, now aged 20, I got married. (Christine and I had 23 years of marriage together and three lovely daughters, but sadly she and I eventually drifted apart as couples do.) I was now in and out of various jobs, but on my 21st birthday I managed to get on a HGV course and I passed. From then on things picked up, and I was driving all over place. I worked on the roads and I worked at Heathrow Airport for eight years. As time progressed I got lots of training driving a whole variety of vehicles, which stood me in good stead for years ahead.

It was some time after I got married and moved to a house not far from where my father had died that I became aware again of the world of Spirit. Little did I realise that my life was about to take on a whole new dimension.

Chapter 2

How My Journey Began

Although the house we lived in during the first years of our marriage was unremarkable in many ways - it was much like the other houses in Beauchamp Road – I began to notice some unusual things about it. There were always floorboards creaking and little things knocking and bumping throughout the house, the sort of things we all experience in life I guess. But I put this down to something entirely different. I sensed it was some friendly spirit, but more than that I wasn't sure.

What also happened in those early years was that Sarah, our first daughter, would often come down in the evening and say she couldn't sleep. Then, when we would take her back to bed she would say, "The lady told me to come down." We disregarded that until much later when I was having a reading from a medium who told me that my grandma used to tell my daughter to go downstairs to mum and dad if she couldn't sleep. So that medium had verified the reason why Sarah used to come down in the evenings on many occasions, and so proved to me that she had undoubtedly heard Grandma. Not long afterwards we moved to another house in Beauchamp Road just five yards from where my father had died after having had that fatal coronary.

So were those creaking floorboards and other familiar sounds Grandma walking the boards and keeping a friendly eye on us? I sometimes wonder. She was certainly with me sometimes over the next few years to inspire and support me, as I will tell you shortly. (Grandma had passed many years previously when I was about 14).

I guess my own journey to becoming a medium really started one evening when my mum asked me if I could give her a lift to the Spiritualist church she sometimes went to in Walton on Thames. "Yes, of course, I will," I said. So off we go and I drive up to the church, and I say to Mum, "What time will you be coming out?"

She says, "Why don't you come in?"

I said, "No, it's alright, I'll stay here and wait." I had never been to a Spiritualist church, so I wasn't sure what it was. Even though my grandma had been a medium I had never being to a Spiritualist church and see her perform. In fact her mediumship was something she kept quiet because my granddad wanted to have nothing to do with it. So when she went out to a Spiritualist church she would say that she was going to a Mothers Meeting. As far as Grandad was concerned my grandmother was an enthusiastic supporter of Mothers Meetings.

So on that fateful night when my mother said, "Why don't you come in," I had no idea what it would be all about, and I didn't really want to be go in. But somehow Mother persuaded me. She said we would only be there for about an hour, so I went in reluctantly with her. She sat in the back row with a friend and I sat at the other end to keep out of sight. My thinking was, 'if I can't see them, then they can't see me.' How stupid is that, now I look back on it. There were a few hymns and a demonstration of clairvoyance, but I didn't really pay much attention. Some people got a 'connection' with their loved ones, but the only connection I was interested in was how long would it be before we could leave. That was more or less all I thought about. I just wasn't aware of how big an impact this night would have on my life.

At last the service was over and I came out of my corner to take Mum home, and politely waited at her side for her to finish talking with her friend. This went on for some time. I didn't know what was going on and I don't think Mum was listening properly either, because what happened next took her by surprise and me as well.

I walked up to Mum and said, "Are you ready,"

Mum said, "Yes I'm ready son," and her friend suddenly looked surprised.

"Oh, do you know this gentleman?

Mum said, "Yes he's my son," and she introduced me to her friend, Gloria.

Then Gloria said, "This is the man I was telling you about, the one with all the energies."

I think Mum was a little confused as I was.

Then Gloria started talking to me about all sorts of things, but I didn't understand what she saying nor why she needed to talk to me. Finally, she said, "Can we have a chat sometime, maybe you might like to come to one of our meditation classes." I politely agreed thinking that would be the end of that.

On the way home Mum explained that Gloria had been a medium, and also pointed out that I, 'the gentleman' hiding at the end of the row, was supposedly giving off energies, spirit energies, and they needed to be used. So I thought, OK I'll meet Gloria again, see what this meditation is all about and that will be the end of that. Or so I thought.

A few weeks later I was invited to Gloria's home to attend

a meditation evening, which was followed by the chat she had planned, during which she persuaded me to attend her meditation meetings for a little while just to see how I felt about coming to the classes. I agreed, as Mum was also going. Eventually my sister Sandra came too.

I was soon enjoying these classes, happy to drift off into meditation, and then share with others what I had been shown in my 'quiet time'. To this day I still don't understand why at times everything I was seeing was in a kind of animated form. Gloria was very helpful as a tutor and we chatted for a long time after the meditation class was over. I also realised that the evening session was referred to as a meditation circle, a class nonetheless!

During my time with Gloria's class we were invited to visit a trance circle. Gloria told us that all we would be doing would be watching students go into trance and noticing what happened. That seemed OK to me knowing that I wouldn't have to do anything, just a free evening. But again there was a surprise in store for me.

Trance is the oldest form of mediumship; it's about allowing yourself to be totally immersed in the energy of a spirit. In other words, the spirit will use you to either teach or connect with others around you. Trance is also used for more physical mediumship, where the spirit's voice takes over and speaks directly to the listeners and where transfiguration takes place (the visiting spirit projects their features over those of the medium). So you will see the medium's face totally change as the spirit projects its own face over theirs. I love watching trance mediumship and have been the host on many occasions.

When we arrived for the trance circle the host was quite strict, giving us very clear instructions, pointing out that we were guests and therefore we were there to observe and nothing more. No interaction at any stage was to be allowed or tolerated, we were to sit in total silence throughout the trance demonstration. 'Suits me fine,' I thought.

The lights were dimmed and we were instructed to relax and let the spirit world perform their work on the trance students we were watching. I tried to keep my eyes open to observe, which I succeeded in doing for a short while. Then I felt so sleepy for want of a better word. I began to hear different kinds of breathing, some heavy, and some light. My eyes began to close, I felt a kind of dizziness which made my eyes close even more rapidly. My heart started to palpitate harder and faster. 'Oh my God,' I thought, 'was I having a heart attack, could anybody see me? 'It is so hard to explain how I felt. I was petrified, I couldn't move, I was really frightened and I asked God for help.

The palpitations eventually got less and less severe but my body felt heavy, and even with my eyes closed, I sensed somebody directly in front of me. Then I heard a voice, saying, "Welcome friend, do you wish to talk to anyone here? It was the trance host addressing me. I felt myself wanting to answer but I couldn't. The words just wouldn't come out. Shortly afterwards, I was able to open my eyes and in front of me was a trance tutor. "You aren't supposed to do that", he grinned. He told me I would feel "normal" very soon and I did.

What had happened was that a spirit had come through me instead of one of the trance students. I had apparently been fighting this trance experience and the way I felt was the result. Once more there was mumbling about me between the tutors.

They were very surprised by what happened, and I certainly was, but not Gloria.

She said to me afterwards, "I knew that was going to happen. All those students have been doing it some months, and you go in first time and you suddenly go into trance."

On the way home everyone else was talking about what had happened and laughing, saying, "It had to be you, it couldn't have been anybody else. "I could see the funny side of it, but actually it was frightening, because I went numb, feeling as if my heart was going to come through my chest. That was how hard my heart was pumping. One of the things you learn as a student of trance is how to control the entry of a spirit, so that you don't have an unpleasant experience, but no one had taught me how to do that because no one expected anything to happen. It was certainly a weird experience. I spent a few more months in the meditation circle before Gloria suggested I should be in a more advanced class, and that she would make arrangements for me to meet a medium friend of hers to 'assess' me. Here we go again I thought.

As promised, arrangements were made and I was sent to a lady called "Madge" who lived in a bungalow in Tolworth, not far away. The meeting was to take place on the next available Saturday morning and I was ordered to be punctual, as Madge was giving up her time for me.

If you ask me why I went it was probably for a number of reasons. I think inside me it felt almost as if someone was taking an interest in me and showing me what I could do. Gloria had taken me under her wing as it were. There was also an element of curiosity; I had experienced a few things in the meditation circle and I had just been to the trance circle, and I thought that was really interesting. I didn't totally enjoy that experience, but it was new and it opened my mind. So when Gloria said, "I'd like you to meet Madge," I thought, 'well what's next.' It was a bit like an adventure, but an adventure that someone else was leading.

What Am I Letting Myself In For?

So I duly arrived at Madge's home. As I approached the front door of her bungalow, trepidation started to creep in. In fact at one point I actually started to leave the garden and headed for the front gate, but the voice in my head was saying, "What's the matter with you, ring the bell". I must have attempted to press the door-bell three or four times before I actually did connect with it, whereupon the front door finally opened and there was this lady with a big smile wearing a lovely summer dress. I introduced myself and she beckoned me inside her home.

"We'll, go straight into the bedroom," she said. 'Oh my God,' I thought, 'What on earth have I let myself in for?' I mean you read about this sort of thing in the Sunday papers don't you? I envisaged all sorts of things, witches, covens dancing naked around the bed. My thoughts were interrupted by a reassuring,"Don't look so worried, we don't bite." "We" I thought, did she say we? Madge then told me of the conversation that she had had with Gloria, and very complimentary it was too!, though the description of my apparent abilities made me question, 'Who? Me?'

At Madge's request I made myself comfortable and noticed the room was very tidy and cosy; the adjoining door was half ajar, so I thought if nothing else, I have an exit route. My host pottered about in the room and put a small glass topped table in front of me, and placed three items of jewelry on it. Madge sat down next to me and asked me to pick up an item of jewelry from the table and I obliged. She told me to take my time and hold the jewelry, "I would like you to read the item in your hand please, tell me everything you feel and see." I learned later that this was called "psychometry", that is, reading the vibration or history of an article by using your own psychic energy to sense the energies being emitted from the item you are holding. Actually, I had done a bit of this before because Gloria would sometimes say to me, "just hold that and tell me what you think." Even so, I didn't feel particularly prepared for what Madge wanted me to do.

As it happened, once I had picked up one of the pieces of jewelry, things began to make themselves aware to me. I was seeing pictures in my head, feeling different vibrations and sometimes feeling ill. At first I was reluctant to share the information I was getting in case it was my own thoughts. Madge, sensing my caution, insisted I share every piece of information that I could retrieve from the object and several times raised her voice and said, "Speak up Roy, we can't hear you". There was that 'we' again. The images I was receiving were sporadic, coming and going and almost fading away before my eyes. Madge interrupted my concentration and asked me to put the item down onto the table and pick up another one of my choice, which I did and started once again to caress the object in my hands. There was no waiting this time, it was like somebody had turned the film back on. Once again I passed the information to Madge, and once again she told me to raise the volume of my voice. I couldn't understand what was going on.

Once this was over I turned to the remaining article of jewelry and asked, "Shall I do this one too?", and she replied, "I wasn't going to get you to do three, but now you have asked." Hey, I was on a roll, she asked me how I was feeling, and I confirmed that I was buzzing, yet a little tired. She said I would get used to it and beckoned me towards the open door of her bedroom. "Some tea I think," she said. "Come through to the front room and meet my friends."

Two ladies came into view as I entered the room. Now I knew where the 'we' had come from, and the request to speak up!. Madge informed me that the ladies were the owners of the items of jewelry I had worked with.

She said to them, "Well what do you think?"

One said, " You picked up mine first."

I said, "How do you know that?"

"Because of the information you gave."

Inside me, I was thinking, wow!

Then the other lady said, "I knew mine was second, it was all so accurate."

Somehow I had left Madge's piece till last. The information I gave her was right too.

So I was really chuffed. I was on cloud nine. We finished our tea, had a long chat and I left the bungalow, elated that I had done the job for which I had being tested. And I kept my clothes on!

They were really nice encouraging ladies, I don't ever recall seeing Madge again to this day. I believe she bought a house in Kent and started up a care home. But I am very grateful for the time she gave me as I gained a lot of confidence from that morning. I received more praise after returning to Gloria's meditation circle, and she topped it off by informing me I was to be offered a place in a developmental circle. "Great," I answered.... "what's that?".

A development circle is a class for mediums and potential psychics. They are usually quite small and you sit in a circle. You are learning all the facts and levels about using your psychic abilities, learning how to connect with your higher self and your sensitivity to other unseen energies. You learn to connect with energies that will enable you to truly use the gifts we have as Earth-dwelling spirits. I guess in a nutshell, it is utilising that which many call "the gift." It is something we all possess, a force that lies buried between ignorance and belief; and believe me, once you tap into this "gift", there are not many who let it go again, because it is the spirit within you, "the real you" that is searching for its own place in your earthly life, yearning to come to the fore to help and guide your physical journey.

Some people would call it their conscience. Remember when you feel like you are struggling to make the right decisions in life and you feel torn between the little angel on one shoulder and the little devil on the other? Well, it's the angel we need to tap into for guidance. Some people do this without any trouble whatsoever. They rely on their own intuition without realising that intuition itself is a psychic energy that is situated in the solar plexus or gut area.

Come And Join Us

Once again I was contacted by someone I had not heard of before; a lovely medium whose name was Margaret Macleese (apologies if I've misspelt your surname, it was a long time ago). I went to her home in Ewell, Surrey for a chat. I was having a few financial problems at home (who doesn't when you are raising a family), so we killed two birds with one stone and I asked to have a reading at the same time. The evening came and I drove to meet Margaret. The only money I had in my pocket was the amount necessary for the reading, and my petrol tank was nearly empty, almost running on air, so I arrived with the full expectation of a four to five mile walk home.

What a lovely lady Margaret was; she was kind and welcoming and one of the best mediums I have met to date. She 'connected' with a number of family members that had passed into the world of Spirit. My dad was very prominent in this reading, only the second time I have ever experienced that. The information she gave me was so accurate it made my hair stand on end, and I didn't have a lot of it to stand up, even then! Some of the information that she shared with me that night was also connected with the second reason I had gone to meet Margaret, which was about my spiritual development. The spirits painted scenes of the spiritual pathway ahead of me. They mentioned that I would teach my trade to others and that I would be a good conduit for connection and guidance throughout the Spirit world. She told me I would heal as well in the years to come, and true to their word, I started practising as a spiritual healer about a year or so later, having already begun healing in the meditation group. Much later in 2008/09 I trained as a Reiki healer, becoming a Reiki Master Practitioner in 2010.

I have to admit that when I heard some of the information about my future, I'd be sceptically thinking "Oh yeah?" However, I learnt very quickly that as thought is the basis of spirit communication, those in the world of Spirit could hear all my negativities. That was something that would haunt me later on in the learning process, and I am still being reminded of this. Margaret continued to amaze me because every time she gave me information about my present life I could relate to it. I was left in no doubt that Margaret was "the real deal".

After the sitting had finished, Margaret suggested I might like to join her own development class. I was pretty excited when she gave me the date and time of the first session. We had a cup of tea and a relaxed chat that seemed to go on for hours. My mind wandered back to the thought of whether I had enough petrol to get anywhere near home. As it was getting dark I brought the conversation to an end; after all, I had a wife and a new baby at home. I also realised that all this time, I had the crumpled £5 note in my hand. I thanked Margaret for everything and gratefully offered her the £5 fee. Margaret refused to take the fee. She told me that she had been instructed by those that had connected with me in the reading, not to accept any gratuity. I was grateful but also proud and insisted she accept her well-earned payment.

Once again she pointed out that she had been instructed by the spirits not to accept and that if I mentioned the matter again it would offend her and that she would refuse to help me further on my new pathway. The conversation ended there, with a big hug of a thank you for the gift she had given me.

As I left Margaret's house my thought returned, 'Will I make it to the petrol station?'. I just about made it. As I pulled into the station forecourt, the engine died on me but I was more than happy to push the heavy car a few yards to the pumps. The Spirit world had helped me get there, but they obviously wanted me to do a bit of work too, so they took me just to the edge of the petrol station, as if to say, "You wanted to get to the petrol station. You're here, you didn't say anything about the pumps, ha, ha." They do have a big sense of humour.

After I met Margaret that day I made a vow, that anytime I was instructed by those in the Spirit world, not to receive a fee. I would honour the instruction. I have to say that I have had the pleasure of returning the favour many times and it is also a gratifying and humbling experience to know that you have been of service.

When the big day came to begin the short journey to learn about mediumship, I was obviously full of nervous apprehension, hoping that I would 'get on' with my new colleagues and hopefully friends. I am happy to say that they have remained friends to this very day and several have continued their journey of mediumship in their own right. I say journey because it is a never ending journey, in this world at least.

Meditation

We were taught meditation once again. It was taught a little differently from my days in Gloria's classes, but no two people teach the same. I was happy with this early stage, owing to the fact that I had had experience of meditation before, and over time meditation has shown itself to be the powerful aid it is, for so many things in life.

Many people see meditation as just something that others do, and they do not understand the benefits of shall we say 'taking time out,' yet more and more people are trying it in different forms. Tai chi is a great meditative tool, slowing down physical and mental movement, giving a person the feeling of being in total control, each move guided and gentle. In this way the body and brain are also taking time out for a meditative session although in the briefest manner. Think of the times the brain places you in momentary 'pause' position. You go into your own trance-like state, you can hear people talking around you, people are waving their arms and hands in front of you and yet you are in this sublime world of peace and harmony, for the briefest of moments. Remember we used to call it "being in a daze?". Everybody should try meditation, even for a short moment in time. The gentle calming sensations help you and your health, and aid sleep, allowing your body to tone down a gear.

Everything in this world takes us at far too fast a pace. Meditation helps us to slow things down, helping us to make decisions and judgments in a more calculated and acceptable manner. I know most people will now be saying, "It's alright for those with plenty of time, I have children to get to school, a job to go to," and so on, or they are simply keeping lives 'on track.' However, as I said, meditation is an aid to your everyday life, not a hindrance. All you need is just a little time, anytime, anywhere, in any place, and you can meditate. You are not going to go to sleep, but simply placing your mind and body in a more acceptable plane, recharging your inner self to deal with the next phases of your day, and being ready for what is ahead.

You do not need to clear your mind as so many have taught before, you just refocus on being somewhere different for a short time. I do not practise meditation at the same time every day, far from it. I do however use meditation before a private sitting or public presentation. I always use it when I feel a little threatened by fear or anxiety, such as when I am at the dentist, or as I remember at the time of an MRI scan, after the radiographer told me I would be immersed in the tube for 30 minutes with "no moving please". So I lay there motionless, and meditated undisturbed by what was going on around me. Even the noise of the machine and background music did not stop me from attaining my happy place; not only that but I had the added bonus of experiencing the feeling that the whole 30 minute scan seemed to me to have only lasted 5 minutes, though of course the hospital clock said something totally different.

You do not need to do the 'lotus position,' just be comfortable in a chair or even a bed, should you be at home. Everybody can achieve some level of meditation, and there are many tutors out there waiting to help. I will add an example of focusing on meditation a little later in this book.

Learning About Mediumship

We spent several weeks, no, months in the throes of learning our trade as budding mediums. Margaret Macleese in my opinion was an excellent teacher and I had already experienced her skills at mediumship first hand, so I knew we were being guided by a true professional. She was firm and fair and a lovely lady and friend. She had a calming, gentle Irish accent. We all progressed at different levels and speeds, like any class really. Some weeks my colleagues in the class would excel at some things and drop back the next and I was no different, though I was determined to make the most of my time learning. I seemed to feel comfortable in my new schooling. We were attending in all weathers, despite coughs and sniffles. If you did have to miss a class through ill health, you missed it terribly and could not wait for the following sessions to 'catch up'. We not only became very close to our colleagues/friends, but also to the spiritual guides and helpers that were becoming very close to us, not only in the circle of learning but in our personal lives too.

To help you understand what I mean by guides and helpers, I will give you my understanding of who they are:

A Guide: We all have a guide, some might like to refer to them as 'guardian angels.' Your guide will stay with you from the start of your journey (your birth) on this plane until your return to the world of Spirit to which we will all return. This guide you may see or perceive as male or female, that is because it is easier to relate to them in our Earthly form rather than in their spiritual cloak.

Some people even know the name that their guide chooses to share with them. Some wait many years to learn this. My own guide always had a very strong presence around me but chose to be elusive as far as his name was concerned. Several times at the beginning of our 'relationship' I would ask his name only to hear him say "a name is but a label and I will not be labelled." He did share early on that he belonged to the Sioux Nation, the Lakota Sioux. As for his name, you will have to wait a while; just like I did! ha ha, because that became an ongoing thing between us. He is a big man, in height and frame, and in times of anxiety, he doesn't hesitate to step forward. He has steered me away from danger on numerous occasions when I have asked for help.

Helpers: These good souls are with you during the different levels of your life. Just like teachers at different levels of your academic life, they help you through their own experience and skills that they share with you with love. 'Helpers' are not with you every day of your life, but simply in those areas of your life where you ask for guidance. We all consciously and sub-consciously ask for help. These same helpers may also return to help you through your life if you continually struggle with the same situations throughout your Earthly journey.

From a spiritual perspective what's important in life are the experiences you have and what you make of them. It's not a question of passing or failing. That doesn't have any significance. That may sound like an unusual statement because in our physical life we are taught to pass all our examinations, work hard and do our best. That sort of education is to help you on your material pathway, to achieve the level of earthly life you require for yourself, but the experiences of your life are your spiritual 'certificates' for want of a better word. These are invaluable lessons that will be of value to you at a later time in your spirit life.

When the time comes that you choose to become a helper yourself, you will most certainly want to help the loved ones you have left upon the material plane, and you will help them by your own experiences accumulated during your Earthly existence. You have to be able to draw upon your own experiences in order to be a good helper. After all, how can you say to your loved ones and fellow human beings "I understand how you feel", I know your pain and frustration if you have not experienced the same thing yourself?

When you call upon helpers in the world of Spirit,

(those that have trod on the Earthly plane with all its vast experiences), the one that comes to you is saying: "I have walked in your shoes, let me help you through my knowledge of this trial or tribulation you are struggling with." Your spiritual helpers are like an infinite library or an endless source of very skilled people (spirits) at your disposal. There is someone to help everybody whatever their level of earthly intelligence or level of understanding and believe me there is a difference. Similarly, one day your experiences of the life you are living now will enable you to be a helper in the Spirit world when you have passed over.

Moving On

Unfortunately our time with Margaret was not as long as we would have liked. For personal and family reasons she needed to 'close' our group temporarily. This came completely out of the blue, so we were all shocked by this 'temporary' closure. Why temporary? Well let me explain: all things must change, therefore all things on our path are temporary, they must progress. Day and night in a sense are temporary as they are succeeded by another day and night, and the old saying "when one door closes, another door opens" is true about everything in life. Nature shows us this with the seasons; spring brings us life, summer brings us maturity, autumn is a time of release into winter, the time of rest for all things. But the winter is "temporary", it is followed by spring and rejuvenation.

We had been with Margaret for some months and our understanding of meditation and our spiritual development had grown very quickly. Of course we were still very much novices, although in our small way we were becoming a little more confident and proficient with the knowledge we were acquiring, and yes, there were times when we would be a little too sure of ourselves and try to race ahead only to be pulled up and shown we were not the budding psychics that we strived to be, budding we hoped, psychics? Well that was a few miles down the road yet.

There we were with one door closing, aware that this part of our journey was at an end. Amidst the sadness and the trepidation, Margaret broke the silence that was holding us. A little glimmer of a smile came over her face. She explained that if we could find another venue, then Spirit would provide an answer for the progression of our learning pathway. We thought to ourselves, where could we go?

My thoughts were, it can't be *my* home, my rented home is not very big and I have a wife and young baby girl there, and there is absolutely no space in which to hold a class. Not only that, the house is not very warm. (The state of repair due to the miserly landlord was poor, so the home was on the cool side in the winter!). So I sheepishly kept quiet.

As I was listening to the conversations of who could or could not hold the circle at their place, the strangest thing happened to me. What happened seemed strange then, but nothing seems strange now after working for more than forty years connecting with Spirit. As all the voices were chatting away it suddenly felt as if somebody had turned the volume down in the room, I could still hear muffled voices but no clarity. You know how it sounds when you go underwater at the swimming pool?, it was just like that. Then I heard a loud but short tone in my ear. Needless to say, I shook my head and tapped my ear, and the tone disappeared, but I heard a soft but strong voice!! The words were quite clear, the words were: "You will take over the chair of this circle."

I am sure I do not need to explain the thoughts that went through my head, probably the words were not even suitable in the presence of our Spirit friends and guides either. My second reaction was not an improvement either,

I told myself that I was having delusions above my station. So the best thing was to just keep my mouth shut and wait to see who our new chairperson or tutor would be. Margaret gave us a few more moments to decide. I felt a bit more relaxed leaving this decision to somebody else, but the feeling was short lived as once again the volume of the conversation decreased and the tone in my ear returned. The voice also returned, with the very same words; my head quickly turned to Margaret looking for some advice, but her look said it all. She just smiled at me and I felt goose bumps all the way down my back. I was in a daydream surely.

Suddenly my daydream was interrupted by the voice of one of my circle colleagues. Beryl Denney spoke up and very kindly offered her home as the new venue for the circle. Beryl's home was situated in New Malden a short distance from my home. Tuesday night was best for her, she lived alone and there would be no pressure on how long the classes lasted. Again my eyes turned to Margaret, and even though she was acknowledging Beryl's kind offer, she was still looking at me with that big 'knowing' smile. It's funny, by now I was having mixed emotions, my fear was that she might know what I had heard from Spirit, and yet her smile was putting me in a better place, a happy bubble as funny as it may seem.

Without moving her glance from me, Margaret then addressed the whole class. "The person that will take over the class has already been informed of this," she continued. Well it didn't take long for the rest of the class to notice that she was staring at me. She continued, "I am just waiting for him to acknowledge the responsibility." "Him", she mentioned, "him", what a giveaway, no clues needed, as I was the only "him" in the room. Thank you Margaret! "OK" I blurted, "I did hear somebody telling me that I would be chair of the circle, but that is ridiculous, I am a student not a teacher and I know no more than anyone else here." Inside my head once more, I heard the voice: "Oh ye of little faith" and the answer I returned?" Well, honestly I cannot remember it, which is probably for the best.

I Can't Believe I'm Leading!

Well it all happened like clockwork, Beryl made her home available, and the day came when we were due to meet. Naturally I was a bit anxious as anyone would be starting in a new role. Yet beneath the fear, was a feeling of pride. I think what also helped was that I was so easily accepted as leader. You might expect some degree of jealousy and ego from those within the circle, but I do not remember any, especially at the beginning. In fact I think we were all as nervous as each other and I am sure that helped the situation.

The thoughts of Margaret, our former teacher were still firmly embedded in us, along with the lessons she had taught us over what seemed to be a few short months. I remained friends with Margaret for many years, I shared the progress of her ex pupils and we put the world to rights over a cup of tea more than a dozen times. Then sadly we lost touch, but now as I reflect on that time of my life I would just like to say from my heart to Margaret Macleese and all those before her who found worth in me: "Thank you for beginning my journey and teaching me how to maintain my roots with the world of Spirit, God bless you all!"

Jumping into a medium's shoes was never going to be easy. In fact, I thought it was going to be impossible, but then we seemed to be forgetting that we were still students in the eyes of the masters and guides in the world of Spirit. They were not about to let anybody falter or fail, and I would be the instrument that they would use to convey their lessons.

Basically I would be guided or 'do as I was told' in a loving kind of way of course.

I am pleased to say that everything came together after a short while in the circle, and everyone's skills went from strength to strength. We were all learning from each other, so it wasn't a case of a tutor and the class; I feel we worked as a team together, and I am sure that moved the level of energies up no end. You need energy to power a light bulb and you need energies to link with the Spirit world, just a different type of energy.

Friendships And Prophecies

We very much became close friends and colleagues and I am honoured to have spent more than two years learning with them. Some of these good people I am still in contact with. I would like to thank them also for being a part of my learning journey, and my spiritual journey. My thanks go to Beryl Denny, Anne Germain, Frances, Jim Campbell and Jane Denny. We had a lot of fun and plenty of chats during tea and biscuits after our class. If anybody had required some spiritual healing, then one of us would gladly supply the energies. During our time together, a number of prophecies were given to us. For example, I saw the demise of the Berlin Wall. The images I was shown are reminding me even today of the accuracy of the Spirit world. They are the very images that I would witness coming from my TV screen some years later. I am to this day, amazed at those images.

May I at this time offer some advice to mediums and students alike regarding prophecy: simply log them with date, time and description. Place them in a sealed envelope and store them somewhere safe, otherwise you will lose the miracle of sharing with the world a prophecy from the world of Spirit. Mine? I should have placed it in a bank each time and then got the bank manager to open it once the prophecy revealed itself. What a great proof that would have been and what an opportunity I missed.

As the circle of friends and students progressed, we invited members of the public to 'sit in' to be our 'guinea pigs'. They were friends, relatives, or people from the local Spiritualist church, they were people to 'practice on.' We had some great nights and how wonderful it was to be able to receive feedback from a stranger. I made a lot of good friends during my years in the circle. One or two left our group for one reason or another and were soon replaced. I believe we generally had a group of seven for most of the time together, and we really were together, and we were tested and educated to be patient and tolerant especially with ourselves.

We learnt to trust each other in more ways than one, we gave and received support not only on our spiritual journey but our physical journey also. After all, so many things were going on in our own lives: divorce, bereavement, everyday challenges and difficulties, but we were 'there' for each other. During our development sessions we also received support and messages from the world of spirit. Things just don't seem so bad after you are given proof and truth from a loved one in the world of Spirit. In my case, usually my dad or Grandma would come through and give me encouragement to get back on track. No different really from their being still on this Earth and myself asking them for advice.

You Can Ask For Spiritual Help Too

Have you ever thought of asking someone in the Spirit world for some help and advice? Did you know this is possible? They are still there for you, putting little ideas into your mind to help. Of course it's up to you whether you having the foresight to follow the advice that seemingly 'comes into your head' and if you don't have that foresight, then don't blame those loved ones in the world of Spirit because you declined their help. If you ask them, you must be prepared to 'listen'; don't expect the answers to come through your ears, it will seem like an inner thought. Don't take my word for it, try it out for yourself.

Trust the results that seem to suddenly fill your head; you will see results. Those results will be like a seed, the trust you have in those of Spirit will grow and you will get guidance just as you need it. But please remember, those loved ones, guides and helpers cannot make your mind up for you, they cannot change 'your life.' The decisions to take advice or guidance is totally yours. It is your own free will to accept, but I must add here that I have never been let down. The words *trust* and *faith* will always be a prominent part of your life when you link with those in the world of Spirit.

I am sure that at some stages of your life you felt that you just had to do a certain thing, a certain way, that someone or something was helping you make that decision, even if you felt it was going against your normal way of thinking. Some of you may say that you just followed your 'gut instinct.' There is in your life so much positive energy that you can 'tap into.' The more positive you are the more positivity you will attract and of course vice versa with negative thoughts and deeds. Worrying about things in our life does not help the problem, it only aggravates us and the situation.

One of the things that I learnt as a medium is that everything is temporary. The things that worry us are usually temporary. I learnt a lot in my two and a half years developing as a medium, and I enjoyed teaching mediumship and helping others to become mediums and perform publicly. Teaching I thought was going to be my main role, but it was soon made clear to me that I was going to be more than a teacher. I was going to go out and give public demonstrations. What a challenge that was!

Chapter 3

Launching Into The World

After those wonderful years of learning in our development circle, in which everyone had done so well, we were getting to the stage where we felt we had to put into practice what we had learnt. I remember saying to the others: "How long do you expect to stay in the circle? We're getting to the point where the bird should leave the nest, you have to put yourself into flight. We are working towards trying to get one or two of you onto a platform." Some time later, during a time of meditation, it was pointed out to me that having helped others to reach the required standard of development my teaching work was done. What was needed now was experience. If I expected others to go out and bring love and light through the experience of connecting with the world of Spirit, then I had to set an example.

Admittedly, at the back of my mind I probably did know that I would eventually perform on a platform, because after I had given that first reading to Margaret all those years ago I did think, 'wow I might be able to do this.' So you could say I was just delaying the inevitable, but I was still in my early

20s, and I had never done anything like this before. A lot of mediums start much later in life.

So I took my courage in both hands and started asking one or two people if they knew of a Spiritualist church that would like to be visited by a new medium. It was my friend Beryl who found a church for me. She said, "I know a church, shall I ask them if they would like you to do a session with someone on the rostrum." Even though I had talked to her about this I wanted to say no, but I said, "Yes you can arrange it." Shortly afterwards the church's Medium Secretary phoned and asked me when I could come. We set up a date for two weeks later.

Having agreed, my worries then went into overdrive. I was thinking, 'Oh my God, this is really going to happen.' Where my mind was at this time I hate to say. Was I ready? Was I capable? Should I emigrate whilst I had the chance? Yet at the same time, my head was filled with messages from the world of Spirit, such as "Oh ye of little faith", and, "Remember the journey of a thousand miles begins with a single step". I knew this was what I had been working for really, to show others that we can communicate with those who have passed over, our loved ones, friends and relatives. I believe I was nervous every single day of the fortnight while I was waiting, My head was full of challenging thoughts as to my capability despite everything that we had been taught.

Well, the day arrived and to be honest, even before I left home, my stomach was going through more cycles than a washing machine. Somehow I had to get myself together and get out of the front door. I felt physically sick at the thought of standing up in front of total strangers. Somehow I managed to drive myself to the venue.

The car journey ended far too quickly, I arrived much too early, and now I had too much time for anxious thinking. So I thought maybe I should try a little meditation. Time passed and eventually another car parked next to me, then another. The committee were arriving, and as if "en masse" they were standing next to my car introducing themselves, but their names would not register in my brain. They beckoned me into the building and showed me into a small room that had a notice saying "Medium's Room". I knew by the end of the evening that all would be revealed as to whether I was in the appropriate room!

We had a cup of tea and they left me to prepare myself for the evening. Every now and then I would pop my head around the door to see how many were in the congregation, 2, 4, 8, hey I can deal with a small party, I thought - no different to working in a circle, Roy come on be brave.

A short time later a committee member came in and explained the timetable for the evening ahead of us. During our conversation I asked her who was the other medium that I would be working with. To my utter dismay, she replied, "Could you do the whole evening for us." I thought 'Oh my goodness.' Eventually our conversation ended and she invited me to join her on the rostrum. I opened the door for her and followed her out into the church, my body shaking. Then I looked at the congregation and I could not believe my eyes! Now there weren't eight people but easily 48.

My daze was brought to an end when another committee member came over to me saying: "Hello, I'm Jane, I will be chairing for you tonight." She continued: "It's a good turn out tonight." I have since learnt that word gets out when there is a new medium demonstrating. Jane asked me if I would open in prayer, which I did. My mouth was so dry, but I managed to create a prayer and after my prayer we progressed through several notices and hymns.

Jane then informed the congregation that I needed to hear the voices of those I was guided to link with, and that a simple yes or no would be required as proof or otherwise of the truth of the information that would be given. There was to be no nodding or shrugging, and no excessive talking amongst themselves as the medium needed to concentrate. While she was addressing the multitude I tried to calm myself by meditating. I tried to balance all my chakras, but to little avail. My legs were shaking violently, I'm not sure if they shook on the outside but they certainly shook on the inside.

When she said, "I will now hand you over," I couldn't get up. In fact I made several attempts to stand but my legs wouldn't support me. My hands were on my thighs, and I think what I must have been doing was pushing myself down instead of pulling myself up. Meanwhile the church was hushed. Everything and everybody was quiet with all the faces of the congregation looking up at me. It was then that I heard my grandma's voice in my head. "Come on son" she whispered, "this is what you have been working for all these years," and I thought 'yes I can do this.' It was only then that I found the strength to stand, a little shaky, well, a lot actually, but I was standing.

My eyes scanned the rows of people looking at me and eventually I felt a click with one person. I knew I was connecting with them, and then slowly but surely I was getting information for them from Spirit. They recognised the person I was linking with and the information that came through. Then there was another and another, and things began to fall into place. Those in Spirit were connecting with me and once again, we were working together. I do not remember much about that night, other than it turned into a good trail of information demonstrating the truth of life after death. I was so happy that the first soul I connected with from the world of Spirit was always cheerful and joking because he set a great vibration for the connections that followed.

The evening eventually came to a close and I was led

back to the Medium's Room. That's what it was like back then: the medium was taken to the small (in most cases) Medium's Room, at the beginning of the service and at the end of service the same thing happened, you were ushered back into the 'pen.' In those days it seemed as if it was taboo to approach the medium. Actually, on my way to the room a couple did say to me, "That was really nice, thank you."

The practice of keeping the medium away from the congregation after a demonstration was about to change, I am glad to say, and I was certainly at the forefront of that change. I got some very funny looks from committee members in some of the churches I went to when I suggested that I'd like to have my well-earned cup of tea out of the "pen" and amongst the lovely people of the congregation. We mediums love the feedback we get, because it's very hard to gauge the clarity of the messages that you have been sharing all night, when all you insist on is a yes or no answer. This is important and really very relevant, because we the mediums are the ones who are bringing the messages of proof that life continues after death. So after a church service, I was happy for smiling faces to come up to me to tell me how accurate the information that I had been giving really was. It was very uplifting even when someone was explaining this to me through eyes of 'happy tears.'

Over the following few days I was pretty pleased with myself, especially as the president of the church asked me if I would be prepared to come back another time. Everything seemed fine, but for a very short while, there was a slight fly in the ointment. I received a phone call from a colleague in the circle, first of all congratulating me on my first demonstration, but then for some reason she said that she needed to inform me that an established medium of some experience had been present at the demonstration and was not impressed with the way I had conducted the evening.

This medium, who was shall we say 'old school' was not impressed, because there had been far too much laughter brought in to what should have been a solemn evening. I immediately thought back to the lovely messages that the happy departed ones had given to their loved ones from the world of Spirit. I recalled one or two recipients of these messages giving me feedback, including one member of the congregation who said that their loved one was always oh so happy, and that my messages and the way I presented them were so accurate of the loved one's personality. The loved one in Spirit was laughing, and that is what I was trying to convey, and this sent ripples of amusement in the congregation.

Unfortunately, I still allowed these negative comments to upset me, and for several days I was in a quandary as to whether or not I actually wanted to go on with this work. Luckily I soon got some more positive feedback. One or two other churches asked me to give a demonstration as they had heard some good things about my evening. My mind was changing for the better.

I decided to be positive, much more positive. I turned around the 'old school' medium's comments, I was now going to be one of the first 'new school' mediums respectfully. The reason that night had been a good night of mediumship was because I had allowed those coming in from the world of Spirit to be themselves. I didn't 'dampen' their love or laughter, I didn't try to suppress the personalities of the souls that came in. Personalities live on in the Spirit world. I cannot change that, our personality is a big part of our spirit, forged by our true selves throughout all our years of experience both on this Earth and the continuity of learning in the Spirit world.

The evening was indeed a new beginning for me and I felt I had scraped through the first test. I started to feel proud that I had achieved something so precious in my life, and that the 'old school medium' had in fact spurred me on. She was a hurdle placed on my pathway. Maybe I should reevaluate it for a moment; was it a "hurdle" or a "gift?" I will nudge towards a gift for which I am truly grateful.

A service or demonstration evening never goes by without me thinking about all those who make it possible: my guide, my helpers and the loved ones' friends and relations that bring in the sweet messages for those in the congregation or audience. I also think of all those who raise the vibration of the evening with their fun loving nature and never-ending tales of the days when they walked upon the Earth amongst their loved ones, sharing their life and their love with them. Hopefully one day when you return home to the world of Spirit you will play your part in giving proof and truth of a life everlasting, and your personality will shine out with the most familiar traits to these loved ones you visit upon the Earth plane.

I am not in a position to change anything that is given to me by the world of Spirit. The words that are given to me by those in Spirit I then give completely to my sitters or clients holding back nothing, changing nothing. This is my promise to all my sitters, and I say that right at the beginning. I do this because I work with the personality of the one who has passed over, and on occasions I will get a small amount of 'fruity language' from the departed loved one. Yes, you heard me correctly. I will give a very short amount of the 'fruity language,' because if grandpa or Aunt Mary used colourful language in their life on Earth and I change their comment to say something like "oh dear" or "oh flip" then my sitter will think, 'that can't be grandpa, he would have said worse than that.'

This always brings a smile to my cheeks as I allow them to be themselves, so that hopefully their traits, mannerisms and information that they share with you will be proof in itself of their everlasting existence and that they truly never leave you. They will truly make you feel that they are in the room with you, which of course they are, and you will share that unique relationship that you once loved. They will speak those words or sayings that you particularly relate to and you will feel their love and vibration, which will show that they haven't changed. That's what all the proof and truth is for, isn't it?

The fact that you recognise them for who they are, those in the world of Spirit are excited that they have that link with you for a short while. Maybe it was them that pushed you towards having that reading, connecting with them in the Spirit world, which most certainly happens. So many of those who come to me say that they didn't really know why they had made this decision to connect with loved ones, they just felt inclined to find out more. Sometimes this happens at a time of a birthday or an anniversary connected with those of the family that have passed over. Of course, it can be that the sitter themselves is at a low point of their life and missing Mum, Dad, Gran or maybe a husband or some other loved one. Many have other reasons such as closure. They need that little extra something to be positive that members of the family in Spirit are still around them, that they are well and not still suffering, as some were in the latter days of their life.

On that very subject here is a little thought for you: all ailments, diseases, cancers and bodily damage, both mentally and physically are of the Earth and your Earthly experiences. They are of the body and belong to your material life: nothing returns with you to the Spirit world which was with you when you were on the material plane.

The body, as we call it, belongs to the Earth and shall return to the Earth "ashes to ashes, dust to dust". Cremated or buried within the soil, your body remains here.

So what *does* happen? When you pass over to the Spirit world there's a new garment for you ready and waiting, which is how one grandfather described his new life to his grieving granddaughter. I don't as a rule give readings to those who are under 18, but if a minor comes with their parent then I give the information I receive to the parent. On this occasion the teenage granddaughter came with her mother, who had particularly asked that her daughter accompany her. Her daughter was having many nights of interrupted sleep and was in poor health, because she was still missing her granddad terribly. Teenagers' heads are filled with so many thoughts and worries as it is, so coping with bereavement can hit them very hard and become another source of anxiety to add to their uncertainties.

During the 'connection' between grandfather and granddaughter the granddaughter asked:

"Grandpa, do you still have the same body? Only Mummy said we buried you to give you a good rest."

The grandfather laughed and said,

"Do you remember when my old truck broke down and couldn't be fixed?"

"Yes."

"Grandpa went and got a brand-new one, with no engine problems and no dents in the bodywork and Grandpa was very happy with it. Well, it's the same with people. When you leave the old world, you get a new body for the new world, a body with no problems or dents."

He went on, "I'm so happy in my new body, I'm so happy in my new world where I can watch you grow up and watch over you and your brother and sister."

The mother contacted me weeks later with some lovely

news. She apologised for having put me under pressure as she put it and then thanked me profusely, saying her daughter had slept "like a log" since her 'connection' with Grandpa and that her eating and health had started to improve dramatically. She told me that when she asked her daughter about the change in herself, she answered, "Well Grandpa wouldn't want me to make myself ill, and I know he is in his new house with Nanna and is happier there than ever."

Those are the parts of my work that I love the best. The daughter recently visited me for the first time as an adult in her own right, and I am glad that she had a great 'connection' and is looking to train to be a counsellor for children who have been bereaved. How awesome is that, especially as she has also become extremely sensitive to those in Spirit. Everything has a purpose and a meaning in life.

Chapter 4

Churches Were My Apprenticeship

After my first public appearance in Walton-on-Thames I got invited to give demonstrations in other churches in the surrounding areas. Word started to spread that I was available for this kind of work and invitations increased well beyond my expectations. During my first year these invitations were all from churches in South London and Surrey, which is my home territory, but within another year I was being invited by churches much further afield. This was both welcome but also a little stressful; my wife and I were bringing up three little daughters and I was working as a lorry driver. So there was a lot going on in my life. It was very hard doing a day's work, only to rush home, shower and set off in the car trying to be on time generally for a 7.30 p.m. start.

I was late on a number of occasions, having to quietly enter a church so as not to disturb the service, and I was frequently embarrassed by the fact that most of the doors of entry to these churches had creaking or squeaky hinges or handles, so that as I entered the entire congregation seemed to turn around in unison to see where the noise was coming from.

However, there was always a big smile and a gasp of relief from the person on the rostrum, who was generally somebody thrown into the evening as a substitute for me by their church committee and who really didn't want to be the centre of attention. Within minutes of my entry I would be on the rostrum trying to find my first link, whilst trying to relax at the same time.

You might wonder how I managed with such a busy schedule. Well, I learnt to conserve my energy and to use my energy properly, which is something one learns as a medium and which is something that we all should learn. I learnt to use three different energies: I learnt how to use my own energy, the Earth's energy, and the Universal energy instead of just my own energy, because if I'm just using my own energy I become drained. When I'm using the Universal energy my energy is replenished time and time again. The Earth's energy is powerful too. It lies at the core of the Earth and we draw upon it every day whether we realise it or not. So I learnt to gauge my energies and draw in the energies that I needed so that I wasn't coming home tired all the time. If I did feel some residual stress, just being with my family would lift me up. No matter what we were going through my family was always there for me, and I was there for them. So that's how I managed to go on giving demonstrations around what I call the church circuit.

The church circuit was really an apprenticeship during which I had to hone my skills to a precision that I would come to rely on much later on. I have been asked whether I was mentored in any way as I ventured out into more and more churches. No, there was no one to mentor me as such. On the other hand, when you go on to the rostrum in a church there is usually another medium sitting in the congregation, and sometimes they will say to you afterwards "that was brilliant" and then you would start discussing your experiences, and the other medium might say, "Well this is what *I* do." One thing I did do was to watch some of my medium friends. I remember there were a couple of ladies whom I knew who were such wonderful mediums, and I would think to myself, 'You are the bees knees, you are so down-to-earth and you're making people laugh, you're putting smiles on people's faces, and your proof of the world of Spirit is out of this world - in more ways than one!"

I've been asked many times what do I remember about those early years. Ha, fear! Fear of getting things wrong, fear of the word 'no,' when I was giving information, fear of someone saying 'no,' when I would say "can you take this." Yet contradictory as this may seem I also felt a kind of confidence in what I was doing. The fact is that it is quite usual for someone to say 'no' when you give them information, because you might be telling them something that happened years ago, and they have forgotten all about it. It's often only later when they have that 'aha' moment that they recognise what they have heard.

If I did have any doubts or worries about appearing on stage I knew there was no way that the spirits would let me down. I had taken a big leap to go from the comfort of being in that little development circle to being out on the rostrum. And I had done that because my guide had said to me, "If you want other people in the circle to go out and demonstrate you have to get out and do it yourself first". In that first year everything seemed to happen automatically: I would go onto the rostrum, give messages, have my tea and biscuits, meet a few people and go home. I was doing the job I felt I was supposed to be doing. I think my confidence grew when I could finish a session in a church, sit by the side of the pews, and have three, four or five people come up to me and say thank you, or that was spot on what you said about my dad, or even that was amazing what you said about my mum. But when I heard that I always thought – and still think – it wasn't amazing that I was doing it, but it was amazing the information that was coming through me. I think any confidence I had was in the Spirit world, it wasn't in myself. So every time I got up there I would think, it's up to you guys in Spirit, tell me, tell me the things I am meant to say.

One skill that all mediums have to learn is working with congregations. Just as in life you come across those that are so easy and genuine where you gel immediately, and then there are others which are just hard work. Most of the congregations I met were happily in the first category, they responded easily and openly to what they heard creating a lovely relaxed energy.

The hospitality of the churches could be quite varied. The majority of welcomes were absolutely heartwarming, a shake of the hand, a hug, and some time to yourself in which to relax, and that would be the case even on those occasions when I was late. That kind of welcome actually raises the energies for the evening ahead. On the other hand there were others, where the less said the better.

I think the worst welcome I had was quite early on in my apprenticeship. I arrived at the church well on time, full of enthusiasm and introduced myself, but I don't think the lady I met had listened to a word I said. She turned her back on me, then turning back to face me, slapped a hymn book on my chest along with a prayer card and bellowed, "You can sit anywhere, as long as it's not the last two rows," adding,"They are reserved for the committee only.

Again I said, "I am the medium." By this time she was

sitting down doing something else. My thoughts were, 'Well at least they know I am here'. Time was moving on, and more and more people were arriving. At about 7:25 p.m. a lady (later to introduce herself as a committee member) walked past me and up to my oh-so-eloquent receptionist, and I overheard her say, "Another medium not turned up then, and no calls to apologise?" There were a few more tuts and she started to head back to the front of the church. I caught her attention and she said, "Unless you are the medium, it will have to wait until after the service". She looked me up and down, I was the only guy there and dressed up to the nines to meet the general public and then it dawned on her who I was. She growled, "What on earth are you doing sitting *there* Mr Mackay? You should be in the Medium's Room preparing." As she closed the door on me her raised voice echoed, "Five minutes Mr MacKay," and then promptly on the fifth minute she came in and escorted me to the church rostrum. It was almost surreal. Thankfully the evening progressed without a hitch.

When there was a more relaxed time afterwards, I explained everything, though it didn't seem to help much as she continued to tell me that I should have spoken up for myself. As I opened my mouth to speak, the door burst open and then my dear friend who had greeted me at the entrance walked in and almost dropped a tray, on which there was a teapot, a cup and a side plate complete with one chocolate digestive. She then left. After all that I just wanted to get out.

Finally I got up, walked out and closed the church doors behind me, got into my car collected my thoughts together, and turned the radio on and I was serenaded by *The Who* singing "I'm free". How appropriate was that! The funny thing is, I never got invited back which I have to say was quite a relief. I would like to reiterate that normally I am looked after and greeted so well, that it is always a pleasure to return to a church. On those occasions nothing is ever too much trouble for the committee members, and there is nothing more welcoming than a hug. I don't require special treatment, I just want to be treated like a human being. I do love working in churches and spiritual venues. We have so many laughs from the many Spirit characters that attend.

I get a real buzz going from one audience member to another with messages coming in from loved ones in the world of Spirit. I love the laughter and the gasps as friends and relatives of those in the audience come in through me with exactly the same personality that they had when they walked upon the Earth. It's really fun when they show themselves to me with all their mannerisms which will be familiar to their loved ones sitting in the audience. For example, they may wring their hands or stroke their chin or use some other gesture which makes them immediately recognisable to their loved ones.

One of the funniest mannerisms I remember was when I was working from a church rostrum and I kept wanting to scratch my right knee and below it. I was trying hard not to do this as I felt it was rude, but because the irritation was so bad I had to. I thought something may have bitten me. While this was going on I was connecting with a lady a few rows away from me, and annoyingly the other members in her row kept giggling and covering their mouths with their hands. I didn't know what was going on. Eventually, the gentleman in Spirit said to me, "Tell her what you are doing my friend," but I declined, and trying to remain professional I continued. Yet again he said, "Come on mate, tell them what you are doing." I gave in and told her what he was saying to me. I said, "Sorry, I think something has bitten me beneath the knee, and he seems to think it's funny". That was it, the whole row erupted with laughter and it took a few moments for them to compose themselves. The rest of the audience were laughing too, but they didn't know why.

The lady in the row with whom I was linking explained with tears in her eyes what was so funny, and the hall fell quiet. She apologised and said that my link with her husband was absolutely perfect. She explained that he had lost his leg below the knee, due to a smoking related condition, but although the knee and what was below it was amputated he continued to scratch the non-existent limb because he still felt an itch, so he would scratch his prosthetic leg. After a while this urge started to decrease. However, this scratching got so many laughs, that it became his party piece. She burst into laughter again saying he used to even get other people to scratch his prosthetic leg for him. The others in the row with his wife were his two daughters and a niece. They all came to me later for private readings, but I have to say, all that scratching wasn't so funny after the second, third and fourth explanation! He certainly raised the energies that night. What a nice guy and a great personality!

That experience is what makes a reading very special: when the spirit brings in their personality in such a way that their loved ones cannot fail to recognise the person they thought they had lost. To hear the recipient of a message say to me and the audience, "Oh my God, you have him to a tee, his mannerisms and sayings were all there, including the little naughty language or swearing." Well, if that was their nature, their personality, then how can I hold it back? I don't, but I restrict the naughty language to the very first part of my communication and then reserve the rest for afterwards in private if that is asked for.

When you develop as a medium your focus is on other

people. You're not getting messages all the time for yourself, your family or your friends. Occasionally you do, and in my experience when that happens it can be very memorable and even miraculous, as I will tell you in the next chapter.

Chapter 5

Mum's Miracle

I have been working as a medium now for more than 45 years, and during that time I have witnessed so many wonderful events and revelations, both in the churches I have worked in and in my private sessions. At the same time I have been guided through many obstructions in my own life and been gifted in many other ways, so that I have become accustomed to the power of Spirit and the guidance that I receive. Yet there was one event, affecting not just me but my whole family, that took me totally by surprise. At the time it seemed a miracle, and still does.

What's the definition of a miracle? There are many of course, but here is one that I think sums it up:

An extraordinary and welcome event, that is not explicable by natural or scientific laws, which is therefore attributed to a divine agency.

I remember very well the whole sequence of events, which all occurred during one month in the mid 1980s. I was watching TV and thoroughly enjoying a gripping drama. While I was engrossed in the film I began to hear a ringing in my ears which sounded like an alarm bell from the Spirit world. It was like hearing a ringing telephone alerting you to the fact that someone is trying to contact you. Much as I love the world of Spirit this particular connection was not very welcome to me because what I was watching was so absorbing, and I didn't want to miss any of it. So I told the spirit communicator, "OK, I can hear you but let me watch the rest of this and I will be available in a few moments," but the spirit wasn't taking that for an answer. There was no 'let up', the ringing in my ears went on and on and became more rapid and clearly more insistent. So I gave in and turned off the TV.

The moment I turned off the TV I heard a man's voice saying, "Your mother needs to see a doctor." Well, that was certainly news to me, because I had only seen her the day before and she seemed perfectly fine. Again they repeated the same words: "Your mother needs to see a doctor." I soon realised that I had to accept what I had heard, but then pondered how on earth was I going to get the message across to Mum. I knew for a fact that her reply to me would be, "Roy, there is nothing wrong with me thank you," and that would be the abrupt end to that conversation. I loved Mum with all my heart and I knew she loved me too, but it always seemed that if anything needed to be suggested to Mum of whatever kind, it came better from my sisters or my brother.

Mum was a very strong, independent woman. She was very much her own person even alongside Dad. She loved him no end, but she would stand her own ground with him. Dad's name was Roy just like mine. I've often thought that when she heard my name she would very probably have been instantly reminded of the other Roy in her life, the Roy she gave her heart to, and the Roy she missed till the end of her life. So hearing my name would always remind her of her loss, and therefore made it difficult for her to really take on board sometimes what I was saying. These are my reflections many years later.

So back to my story. I contacted my sister Sandra, and passed on the message that I had been given, and Sandra said she would talk to Mum. Even with my sister relaying the message I still wasn't sure that Mum would 'play ball.' Somehow Sandie waved a magic wand and an appointment to see a doctor was set up. Needless to say, I was very anxious and nervous about what the result would be.

Mum duly went to the doctor and nothing out of the ordinary was found, so there was a sigh of relief throughout the family, though at the time I was a little embarrassed to say the least. This incident really started to confuse me and test my belief in what I receive from the world of Spirit. All sorts of questions entered my head, such as how could I get it so wrong, and why would I be given wrong information, especially information that would cause concern for all the family? I didn't have an answer at that time, neither did I have an answer as to why this message was repeated, not only a second time but a third time. Yes, amazingly Mum paid three visits to the doctors' surgery to receive the same result each time that no problems had been found. What must everybody be thinking of me? I had passed the message on through my sister Sandie and somehow she had persuaded Mum to attend the doctors' surgery three times. It was remarkable that Mum did so. I was still left wondering, what is going to happen now? Are there going be even more warnings?

No more warnings were necessary, because our GP, Doctor Brown, a highly respected doctor in our community, had been thinking about Mum's case. He knew that on the surface there was nothing seemingly untoward about Mum's condition, but for reasons that we will never know he had a sense that something might not be right after all. So he decided to make an appointment for Mum to go to the hospital in nearby Kingston-upon-Thames for further investigations. My sister Sandie took Mum for her appointment. Mum was taken in for a check-up whilst Sandie stayed in the waiting room.

Shortly after Mum had been taken into the consulting room, the specialist came out to see my sister and told her that Mum had several problems, one of which were polyps around her heart. So he was sending her to St George's Hospital, in South London, which is known worldwide for its cardiac and neurosurgery work, for further investigation and very probably an operation.

Mum, ever the independent one, said she didn't really want to go, especially as she had no clothes for an overnight stay. How much she had been told about her condition by the consultant is hard to say – probably not a lot so as not to alarm her. So she may still have been thinking that everyone was just fussing. After all, as far as she was concerned she was OK. Eventually, Mum gave way after she had been allowed to go home and pick up a few things on the understanding that as soon as she had done that she must go straight to the hospital.

Mum went home with Sandra, got hold of what she said she needed, and then did something that was characteristic of her. With a rush to hospital ahead of her, she went upstairs and lit up a cigarette! But not for long. After a few puffs my sister caught her out. "Mum, we've got to go now,!" my sister said.

Mum replied, "OK, I'm ready, I still can't see what all the fuss is about."

Not long afterwards Mum was in for a big surprise, as were we all.

After seeing a specialist Mum was told that she would be

having a heart operation within 24 hours. It wasn't just going to be a routine operation but a triple bypass. Apparently, her artery problems were so severe that the specialist could not believe that Mum was 'still standing upright.' We learnt later that Mum was one of only a few females that had been given that operation at that time, when triple bypasses were still relatively new.

Those traumatic hours of waiting for Mum's operation, then waiting to hear how it went and then waiting for the time when we could visit seemed to drag on and on. Eventually we were allowed to see her. For a lady that had been through such invasive surgery she was pretty chirpy. As so often with her, she was amazing, so resilient, and of such good heart.

During her stay in hospital, I took every opportunity to give her healing which allowed her to leave hospital several days early. The doctors and nurses were amazed at her recovery, and I was grateful to them all, not only for the care they gave her, but for their open minds, allowing me those healing sessions with her. We were also grateful to those unseen voices and medical people from the world of Spirit who gave their love and time for her wellbeing and gave her an extended life, at least that's how we saw it.

Whether she was changed by that experience is hard to say. Mum never spoke about anything to do with the operation; she just went on with life pretty much as before, always busy with something and always with a smile and a laugh. However, I'm sure that Mum's mother, who was a medium, would have been talking to her at some stage and saying to her, "Realise that you have been given a gift, the gift of more life," because Grandma was always saying "make the most of it." So I think Mum may have had a little more in her step afterwards, because maybe the operation showed her that she needed to slow down a little bit, and realise that life wasn't just about waiting for Dad to come back. One thing that did change - she stopped smoking. She lived another ten years.

Chapter 6

Busier and Busier

My work as a medium developed quite rapidly after the first couple of years, so that within four or five years I was working across a 100 mile radius of my home across many counties: Surrey and South London, Hampshire, Sussex and Oxford, as well as Essex, Kent and Dorset. My life got wider and wider just like my waist! Wherever I went I was offered tea and cakes and biscuits, and who was I to refuse?

The churches I served, some of which I still work in, were a major part of my spiritual development as they still are. All the churches have their uniqueness and they treat me in their different ways, but one thing has remained the same all these 45 years, and that is the pride and nervous feelings I get when I land on stage.

From that first day when I stood up to give my first service to the present day I am still so nervous, sometimes to the extent that I feel physically sick. Oh I am getting used to it, so much so that I tell myself that if the nervous part stops, then it will be time for me to give up this spiritual pathway. Why? Because I believe that like an actor, once I am no longer feeling that apprehension, then I am opening the door for my ego to take the reins which would sooner or later let me down. So I pray each day that I will always respect the fact that I need to try and keep humility in my work, and remember that the 'great' part of my work is done by unseen eyes and bodies.

Don't get me wrong, I love the audience and clientele telling me that I "rocked the place", which happened to me recently, and that I was in control from the very first connection. It was wonderful to see their faces when I told them that I was shaking in my boots until we had found that first Spirit link. So it's good to know that I look confident. Maybe there is a little showmanship underneath, but it is well tucked away. I know in my heart that what I do on the rostrum – and in private readings for that matter too – is done through Spirit and I pray that I remember that.

As time progressed I became more fluent, more comfortable in working from the rostrum. I didn't have to think what do I do next, and it became easier and easier to switch from giving a message to one person and then to another or switching from being the medium to leading the prayers or giving a short Spirit-guided address. Throughout all this time I was making many friends, some of whom are now very close to me.

A Full Life

As I look back on my time as a medium, especially the first 20 years, there was so much going on in my life that I wonder now how I managed to fit it all in. I was a lorry driver in the early years driving mostly from Surbiton to towns along the Sussex coast and back in a day, and I had a young family. I'd usually be out of the door by 6 a.m. or 6.30 a.m. and on a good day I'd be back by 3 p.m., but on a not so good day I'd be home by 6 p.m. Later on in my life I worked at Heathrow Airport which was better.

It could be quite tiring keeping down a full time job, rushing home, grabbing a sandwich, kissing my wife and kids and then shooting off to drive through the Home Counties in heavy traffic in order to arrive on time. Obviously I was expected to arrive before a service started, but sometimes that didn't happen through no fault of my own. Inevitably there were times when my lateness annoyed those who were organising the church service, but you just learnt to take it in your stride and look forward to the journey home, where I could have the most peaceful time of my day.

My work with the churches varied, but I was usually working in a church a couple of times a week and still am. I would generally be in a church for Sunday divine service, I might also do a Saturday 'special,' (supper and clairvoyance), or I might do an evening of clairvoyance on a Wednesday or Thursday. The Saturday specials or 'psychic suppers' as they were also known were usually to raise money for the church or for a charity. So it was quite a full life with family and friends to think about as well.

I only ever regretted working in the churches when the summer came, because all the barbeque invites were on a Saturday or Sunday, and I had to be on the road just as the party was warming up. Autumn and winter could be pretty hazardous with storms and snow; generally I was travelling at peak times, so to say the least I might arrive at my destination sometimes in a pretty stressed condition, but the show had to go on, and it did!

You might ask why did I do so much? Well, once I started the medium work I couldn't let go of it. It was a bit like a drug. When you are working for Spirit and you're working with people in churches you see all sorts of emotions. You touch one person's heart and they are in floods of tears because a message from someone they loved has moved them so deeply. Their mother or father, or their brother or sister or some very dear friend they have lost speaks directly to their feelings, and tears flow. Then the next minute you're talking to someone else in the congregation and the messages you bring them send them into fits of laughter, and sometimes the whole congregation laughs as well. And then after the service even the people who have been crying come up to you and say thank you so much. There have been times when people have said to me, "You don't know what you've done, you've changed my life." To think that you have changed someone's life – albeit with the help of Spirit – is amazing and it is so heartwarming. So I couldn't stop, but it was more than that. I was still on a learning process. I was meeting other mediums, some of whom had been doing this for 10 years or more, and I felt I still had more to learn.

Once I was on the rostrum and I could feel the energies of the spirits working with me I would be pacing up and down the rostrum and I would be all set to go. I cannot stop still for long, because the energy is there within me. I have to keep pacing, going left and right, forward and back. It's a mixture of my energy and all the anticipation of those in the Spirit world standing behind me. I always apologise to people in advance, and say, "To those of you who don't get a message, this evening is going to look a bit like a tennis match, I'll be going this way and then that way and then back again."

I have to say this, because I watch people and I can see what they're thinking.

They wonder why I'm not standing still or whether I am alright or even whether I will fall off the rostrum! No, it's just the energy inside me. And anyway, all that walking also keeps you alert.

Many people have asked me if I am exhausted after a presentation. Not at all, because the energy I am using is not mine, it is provided by Spirit. The only question I used to have in my mind was, I must be pacing miles every month so "why aren't I slimmer?" Maybe it was to do with the biscuits and cakes I consumed after each service? Perhaps I needed a few more years of pacing the boards, because today I am finally slimmer.

The Unending Support Of Spirit

As I recollect all those years as a medium and all the many people I met and all the different places I went to one thing has remained a constant: while I had many lessons to learn, many trials and tribulations to experience in my Earthly life, my Spirit work never seemed to falter. The Spirit world always had a way of getting the show on the road, as it were. Even through my times of low or ill health.

Whenever I was due to present on a church rostrum or at some other venue and I wasn't feeling 100% in myself, I would ask for divine advice as to whether or not I was fit enough to travel and go ahead with the demonstration. If I was feeling sorry for myself, my Spirit guide and helpers would draw close to me, especially when I was just about to call my venue to cancel. Some might call this conscience, but I would hear this voice that would say to me, "You can't let all those people down, there might be one person who will be there that needs the information and guidance that you can give them." Many times I called this blackmail, only to apologise for my remark under my breath.

The second trick, if they will allow me to use that word to describe something else that they did, which in its way was magical, was what I called their vanishing trick. I wish I had £10 for every time this happened to me. On many occasions I have travelled to venues to give a demonstration streaming with a cold or flu, and on one occasion laryngitis. I would sit at the side of the rostrum waiting for my cue to start, and then once I was invited to begin I would take a few moments to start 'linking in', drag myself up and ask for the audience to send a little love my way in order to get me through the evening, because I was unwell. I was usually coughing anyway, so I think they could see that I wasn't in the best of health. Then something magical used to happen.

Within seconds of linking in to Spirit, my voice would return, the coughing and runny nose would subside and the whole evening would go along as if I were the fittest person alive! That even happened on the evening when I arrived at the church with laryngitis. I was barely able to speak when I arrived. When I asked if there was a microphone I was told, "Yes there is but it's not working at the moment". So I began, and within minutes I was speaking easily and smoothly as if sweet honey had been poured down my throat.

Hence the vanishing trick: now you feel ill and now you don't! Yes, it was a fantastic experience and still is. However, the downside to this is, once all the work of linking with the Spirit world has finished, so the 'vanishing trick' ends and all my symptoms return. Yes, I did wonder many times, if they can do this temporarily, why not permanently?

Well, they place me and other mediums working on stage inside a sort of bubble, a sphere if you like, that separates me from my material body and puts me in a 'spiritual, no man's land', where I am released from the pains and pressures that belong to the Earth plane. Obviously, this energy is temporary, granted to me to complete my session of connection, and the energy is very temporary I can tell you. It leaves me as quickly as it arrives. As soon as I walk out of the church and down the steps to my car all the symptoms of the cold or the flu return. It is quite astonishing, and although I continually moan about this, I have to admit it's a fantastic gift they have shared with me on numerous occasions. So, for all the complaining, I thank them from the bottom of my heart for those ultra-special moments given to me with pure love and intention. The Spirit world is strong, even if the shell of this human being is weak. It is yet further evidence that once we leave this Earth we are free of all physical ailments.

The other constant in all my years of working in the name of Spirit is that each link I get is very different, as different as the many needs of those upon the Earth who are receiving the messages that I give to them. Every person I connect with is as different as our fingerprints or DNA. Our needs and wants are different, as is our levels of understanding. So although it's easy to think that a message or connection is much the same as another, that just isn't so. Our understanding, our intelligence, our beliefs, are personal to ourselves, so one person's interpretation of information will be different from someone else's.

So a time of connection is more intricate than we may well realise. I have been approached many times after a service where two siblings for instance are debating the message that one of them has received. One of them will say, "I think the message received meant etc." and the other will say, "I received it as meaning something different etc." I always say it is for the recipient to understand and not for anyone else. Spirit messages I believe are tuned to the recipient, messages cannot be exchanged, they have a specific destination. And messages are given in keeping with the receiver's level of understanding.

What I also see is that those in the Spirit world have much the same personality as they had when they were on the Earth plane, though their vibrational energies might be changing or have changed. For example, when I am on a rostrum or giving a private reading, there will most likely be a group or gathering of spirits that want to connect with the person I'm talking to, but they will all be behaving differently. Some will be shy, reluctant to come forward too soon whilst there will be others who will come in more strongly and move to the front of the queue. So you might have Aunty Joyce who would love to say hello but she doesn't want to push herself forward. She is like the person at a hotel door who says to others, "Oh no, after you," and she's still standing there ten minutes later. Meanwhile everyone else has gone ahead. I have a client who comes to see me, and as soon as I have linked to Spirit his mother comes in first before everyone else and invariably she makes sure that she is the last one too.

There is also another important aspect to this that is very often overlooked. Even when someone does not understand some piece of information, no matter how many attempts they make in trying to make sense of it, they will eventually understand its meaning. Many people have written reviews of my work saying, "I was not sure at first how to accept the information, but it has become clearer now and I fully understand the logic of the spirit messages." It is my experience that the messages from loved ones in the world of Spirit always find their way home.

I can generally tell whether my connection has hit home. I look for the emotion in the recipient. My motto I guess, is that if I see a tear or a smile, then I have done my job. I certainly do see plenty of smiles and many tears of acceptance showing me that they know without a doubt that for some short moments of time, they were with their loved ones in the Spirit world.

The Spiritualist churches have played a big part in my life, and I have seen many changes in my 45 years on the rostrum. I have seen the way some churches have changed as their committee has changed, sometimes for the better, but unfortunately sometimes for the worse. Some personalities are very strong and like to make their own mark on the church. I suppose you could call this 'church politics,' which is something that I keep well out of. My opinions are my own and not for dissecting or throwing back at me, and I have had to make that abundantly clear to some on my journey. But those have been in the minority, I am happy to say.

Private readings have also played an important part in my life, and I have been doing them for almost as long as I have been appearing on a rostrum. For many years I did them free of charge. When I tell people that today they are surprised. The number one reason why I didn't charge was that I wanted to gain more experience, and the only reason why I changed was because somebody said to me that they would have come to see me earlier if I had been charging. Their thinking was that if you don't charge then you are not very good. Something obviously prompted him to see me all the same. From then on I did ask for payment.

I was still in a quandary however. How much should I charge? I asked the Spirit world for advice and I was told by my guide "man is worth his labour." But that still didn't get me much further. So I decided that I would ask for a donation. The message I got from Spirit was that asking for a donation was not the way to go forward, but that is what I did for a while. I eventually learnt the error of my ways, because asking for a donation confused some people. Whereas most people would just offer what they could afford or what they thought they should others would say, "OK, how much is a donation!" So after a few years I came up with a set fee, which has gradually increased. I love doing private readings; animals as well as people turn up as I will explain in a later chapter.

With so many public appearances, private readings plus

my day job, my life was pretty busy in those early years. So you may be wondering how did I relax? I think it was in two ways: family life and fishing. My family brought me joy and peace of mind, and we would have days away together on the coast, a day here, a day there. And there was always fishing to help me unwind.

I would fish with two of my friends or sometimes on my own. I preferred to go with friends but if they were busy on that day then I would go off on my own. I would fish in a river not too far away and be at one with the river and with Nature all around me. If I wanted to go sea fishing I generally went with half a dozen people. And I still do that. We would pay for a boat and stay out all day, then we would bring back all kinds of different fish.

I remember a funny incident after one of these fishing expeditions. One day we came back from Newhaven and I brought home some rock salmon to gut and put in the freezer. Next day I was in the kitchen degutting several fish, trying to peel back the skin and separate the head on one of them, when I suddenly heard screaming from the garden. I couldn't work out what it was. My middle daughter had taken a fish head out of the kitchen and she was chasing my youngest around the garden with this head making it look like it was going to eat her.

Fishing was very much part of my life. Some of my fishing companions and I would go down to the local working men's club, sometimes on a Saturday and always on a Friday. I'd always go on a Friday because that was when there would be a darts competition, and I was good at darts. There were meat prizes for the winners, and generally I used to win one. Every time I came home my wife would say, "OK, what have we got for dinner today," because she knew I would usually bring home a joint of meat.

Was someone in Spirit helping me to win at darts,

because they knew it was hard for us to make ends meet? I'll never know. When you are a medium all sorts of things happen to you quite unexpectedly. Sometimes they almost take your breath away. And some of the things you see and experience you never forget, which I will tell you about in the next chapter.

Chapter 7

My First Spirit Rescue

In the first five or six years of my mediumship my work was geared towards churches and special functions, such as clairvoyant suppers, where I was working with large numbers of people, and I was also giving talks and doing private readings, but my work was about to take an additional and hugely different track, one that I could never have expected. I call it my "spirit rescue" work.

With spirit rescue work you are helping a spirit that seems to be trapped in this world, that needs Earthly assistance and spiritual guidance to leave and move to the next world. This is not a simple and straightforward process. Very often the spirit of the departed person does not want to leave this world. They may feel that there are things that they would like to see finished, or they feel a very strong attachment to a particular place or to particular people whom they knew when they were in their physical bodies. Sometimes they are quite simply lost. So they have to be helped to pass through this world into the next whether or not they agree to it. Why? Because they are affecting the life and progress of those on the Earthly plane.

The behaviour of a disembodied spirit can be beneficent or malevolent. In popular culture it is the malevolent spirit that is most frequently focused upon, and it is usually in that context where the word exorcism is used. I prefer to use the phrase spirit rescue, because whether the spirit is behaving nicely or not the requirement is the same: the spirit needs to be rescued and released from this world into the next where they will be at peace. The story I'm about to relate to you concerned some very unpleasant activity by a departed spirit, but thankfully it has a happy ending.

After a Sunday evening church service, a committee member asked me if I could spare a few moments to talk with a lady who ran a care home. I hardly had time to think before the lady joined me in the Medium's Room. She was quite pale in the face and she explained that she had not attended the service but had waited until the service was over in order to speak to a 'psychic.' We sat down, and she began with some words that I have so frequently heard down the years and still hear to this day.

"I know you are going to think I am mad," (yes those were her very words) "but I run a guest home for the elderly in Thames Ditton," (local to the Spiritualist church I was working at).

She told me her story concerning a resident of the home. I listened as she explained nervously that there was a spirit in the home that was physically hurting this over 80 year old resident, and she had even recorded the bruises left by the spirit entity on the lady whom we shall call Jane for the sake of anonymity.

Apparently, the care home manager, had approached other 'psychics' and also local clergymen for help, but nobody would give her five minutes to explain what was happening and they would often stop her abruptly saying,"We do not work in that line, you need a specialist."

No one offered any advice as to where she might find that so-called 'specialist,' so she took it into her head to visit a Spiritualist church, not really knowing what to expect but obviously hoping that someone would be able to help. That someone turned out to be me.

As I listened to her I had to smile, considering the few years I had been practising as a medium, because I felt I was probably still 'wet behind the ears' to coin a phrase. Frankly I wasn't sure what I could do, and the care home manager may well have sensed this. She pleaded with me to at least listen to Jane's story and decide for myself as to who would be the right person for the job. I agreed to visit Jane the very next day at the residential home in Thames Ditton, which was only a few miles from my home. At this stage all I could think of was getting advice from somebody who would be experienced in this line.

I contacted as many people as I could, including friends of mine in Spiritualist churches, who might possibly be able to help or who might know of someone who could. I would never have expected the negative replies I had nor the lack of them when I left a message on someone's phone. Again, just like the care home owner, I had people telling me, "It's not my field," or "You need to find a priest." One gentleman hung up the phone as soon as I mentioned physical interaction with this spirit. Eve when I asked people to come with me, see the old lady and show me how to sort this out they still said no.

The next day after work I sat thinking, worrying even. It is quite a big jump from channeling messages on a rostrum to dealing with a nasty disembodied spirit in someone's home. This was something that I had never done before and for which I had no training. So there I was ruminating on what to do. I had been told that the old lady was so frightened and so physically hurt by what was happening to her that she no longer wanted to live. So someone had to help her, but was that meant to be me?

I could feel my guide, 'Grey Wolf,' around me. I meditated on my problem and felt the strong energy of Grey Wolf draw close. I have to say, I felt lost and a little out of my depth. I asked my guide why I felt this way about helping this lady. I admitted I knew nothing of the path I was about to tread that night. He told me that I was feeling the fear that existed in others, how it was blocking the internal and spiritual energy needed to help another soul. He asked me to calculate if my desire to help was strong in me. He asked me if I would stand up for another if I were challenging a physical soul instead of an unseen foe. I still wasn't sure what to do, but I knew that I needed to at least talk to this lady. Grey Wolf told me that I would make my own decision once I had connected with the one who sought our help.

Grey Wolf was very much with me that evening, so let me tell you a little bit about him and how I came to know that he is with me. Grey Wolf is a Lakota Sioux. The Lakota Sioux are a Native American tribe. I wasn't aware of him at first, but shortly after I started on my path to becoming a medium I was sitting in a Spiritualist church and the medium who was on the rostrum that evening said to me, "Are you doing this kind of work, because if not you soon will be," and I replied, "I'm starting to." Then the medium said to me, "Are you aware that there is a Native American who is with you here?" I said, "I don't feel anybody at the moment, but since I was a kid I always loved anything to do with Native Americans", and then the medium said to me, "Well, he is standing right behind you, and I believe he is your guide. He's not giving me any name at present, but he is a very big guy, much taller than you with his hand on your shoulder.

He is towering over you, he is that big. You're not a small person yourself. So you can imagine, he is quite a big guy."

Sometime later I went to an evening of psychic art at another Spiritualist church, where there was an artist creating portraits inspired by Spirit. Just as I was leaving the artist said to me, "I have something for you", and I said, "Why do you have something for me?" He then handed me a portrait that he had drawn of a Native American Indian. He said to me, "That has been with me all evening, I believe it belongs to you, and I believe he is very close to you." He added, "Sometimes people like me do these portraits in advance, and we keep them until Spirit says, "This is the person I want you to give it to."

It was years before Grey Wolf would give me his name. He once gave me a poem while I was watching television, not exactly the best time! But he wouldn't stop, so I turned off the TV, listened and wrote it down. It is very direct and wise, which is what he is himself. He is very down-to-earth but also with a sense of humour; he loves to play jokes on me from time to time. So that's a little about Grey Wolf.

On that memorable Monday evening I realised that the least I could do would be to meet this frightened old lady. So, off I went. I arrived at the residential home in the cold wet winter's evening, wishing I was at home. I meditated for a few short moments whilst in the car, I noticed a light at a window and curtains being drawn. I knew then that my presence had been noticed and it was time to go in. Before I had the chance to press the bell at the front door, it was opened by the lady I had spoken with the night before.

Without saying a word, she led me into Jane's room, the lady that had been experiencing the physical attacks. I was introduced to her as she sat down at her dining table. She gave me a nervous smile and introduced herself to me. Jane was about medium height, a little plump and with beautiful silvery blonde hair. She was very nicely presented, and she was obviously someone who looked after herself. She seemed a sweet natured lady, kindly and softly spoken.

She apologised for not getting up to greet me but explained that she was physically exhausted from all the nights of very little sleep and the physical abuse that she was being subjected to. She kept saying to me, "You must think I am out of my head, but I am not, honestly". I assured her that nothing could be further from my mind. I asked if she would explain to me what had been happening to her. She told me that she was being physically abused and that she had the bruises to prove it. She looked to the care home owner, then proceeded to roll up her sleeves to the elbow. As she did so, it became clear that bruises were present, and that they were at different stages of bruising. Some marks were light and new and other areas were fading. To be honest I was taken aback and I am sure it showed on my facial expression. I had to ask her if she was in the habit of falling. The care home owner interrupted and said that Jane had had one or two falls in the past but had never had this kind of bruising. Part of me became angry that this sweet, frail old lady was being subject to all this bruising. I asked her if she could explain to me in her own words what was going on.

She told me that she had visits during the night several times a week from an old gentleman that appeared in her bedroom. She said that he came from the corner of the room and on occasions there would be one or two women who would come with him. They followed him in and they would be quite rough with her. She told me that they held her down, and that the man would stand at the end of her bed with his arms flaying as if instructing them what to do, whilst making gestures like wringing or washing his hands.

I asked Jane if she had ever jumped up and run out of the room? She replied that the ladies holding her were strong as oxen. She said, "Of course I used to fight, but in the end I felt I would just prefer them to do what they did and leave". "I just want to die" she continued. "I can't fight any more." She asked me if I wanted to see the bruises to her thighs and groin, but the care home owner interrupted saying, "it's not necessary Jane, I have explained to Roy where the bruises are and how you got them. He believes you." After she had told me all the facts, she kept touching my hand and asking me, "You are going to help me Sir, aren't you?"

All I could do was try and gather my thoughts, I could feel my heart pumping fast. Again she described that this had been going on for weeks and weeks. She was embarrassed and felt dirty, she felt she had lost all her self-respect. Jane continued that she was a widow and had always felt her deceased husband's spirit around her, but she had not felt him since all this had started. She felt he must be ashamed of her now, but I managed to talk her out of that train of thought by telling her that loved ones in the Spirit world are sometimes busy etc, etc.

After all this explaining it suddenly hit me that I had never dealt with anything remotely like this before and my mind drifted to the thought that I would have to contact somebody with experience in this field. Oh I had experienced poltergeists and seen objects move on their own or be thrown by a spirit, but physical abuse was totally different.

I reiterated that I might need to find somebody more experienced in this field than I was, and as I was explaining this, Jane broke into tears and insisted that I didn't believe her and said that she just wanted to die. This was heartbreaking, but I was still in a quandary as to what I could do. We continued the discussion for a little longer, and I asked her in which room the incidents were taking place and she pointed to an adjacent door. I asked for a little bit of peace whilst I connected with my guide and helpers. I have to admit, I was feeling pretty ill by now with all the graphic information and proof that I was being given.

I asked Grey Wolf to help me make a decision. Unfortunately his reply was, "This is your decision my friend." I asked him, "What if I make this worse?" His words that returned were words I shall always remember. "The forces of light shall always destroy darkness. This light my friend is at your disposal, do not allow your material fear to control your decision."

I said to Jane that I would need her to come into the room with me. She started to get upset, saying she couldn't and that she now stays clear of it. Several times she said no. I explained to her I felt I needed her to trust me then, as this was the first time I had even met her and that I was entering her bedroom on my own where all her belongings were. She told me she trusted me and she could not accompany me. I agreed to enter the bedroom, totally oblivious as to what might happen. I unlocked the door and went inside, closing the door behind me. I stood at the side of Jane's bed and asked for help from Grey Wolf.

At that moment I felt a weight on my shoulder, just like somebody trying to give me a reassuring touch that all would be fine. I wished I really felt that! I was shaking literally! I decided to ask for a prayer to cleanse the room and remove all negativity therein. Grey Wolf told me I would need to connect with the soul or souls in order to draw them into my light and vicinity. 'Oh great,' I thought, 'I'm bringing the problem towards me. That's a nice idea.'

I called upon the souls that were present and commanded them to leave this world and move into the new world that was awaiting them. I reminded them that they were breaking all the rules (for want of a better word), interfering with the life of those on their material journey. Again I called on them to hear my words. After a few moments I felt the pressure on my shoulder increase. I was beginning to think that was all I had to do, but I was wrong.

Then I heard something, but I did not know what! My eyes were drawn to the far left hand corner of the room. It looked as if smoke was billowing from the corner. Then from the left hand corner the room seemed to expand outwards. Were my eyes deceiving me?. That part of the room was getting bigger and bigger, and I swore I could see movement. I soon realised that I had, because a tall thin man emerged from the smoke standing in the room. As he took a few steps forward there were more figures entering behind him, but these were women. The gentleman wore a large brimmed hat with a hatband. I noticed a lace type collar and the trousers were like "bloomers" for want of a better description, but they were cut short of his shoes. My mind immediately went back to my pictures of the Pilgrim Fathers in the early 17th century. He carried a book in his hand as they were often known to do. The ladies had long dresses on and again a lace type collar. They all wore tight fitting hats which I can only describe as a kind of bonnet in creamy white. The ladies' heads were all facing downwards as they stood behind the gentleman. They were evidently under his influence. He was a very intimidating figure even to me, even though I knew he wasn't real. He made it very clear that he didn't want me to be there, swearing and using offensive language.

I know this sounds strange, but at first I thought he was a clergyman, with his hat partially obscuring his worn face. However, I soon thought otherwise. I noticed that the temperature was getting colder by the minute. It came in blasts, as if somebody kept opening and shutting a fridge door. I was still shaking. As he looked up, I could see a large nose and a pockmarked face, and I felt an enormous shudder move through me. I commanded in the name of Jesus Christ, that they leave this house and move into the light of the Spirit world where they could continue their own spiritual progression, where they could be with those members of their own family that had gone before them. At this point he turned to the women as if to give them instructions to stay where they were. He was being challenged and clearly didn't want to be moved.

In my mind I could hear him laughing condescendingly. For a moment, I lost my track and let my feelings interfere. I called him a bully and a thug, that he could only pick on poor defenceless people that had not the strength to fight back and that his followers were only there out of fear. None of the women raised their head at my accusation. They were mute, either too cowed by the gentleman to say anything or too much under his spell to be conscious of what was going on.

Negative spirits entering the room

Meanwhile the gentleman was moving around in what felt like a freezing, hazy, fog.

One moment he was at one side of the room, seconds later he was somewhere else, and I lost sight of him, but I felt him. I felt his face directly in front of mine, there was a feeling of nose to nose confrontation. The front of my face was enveloped in a freezing cold that is hard to explain, it wasn't a normal cold.

I told him I was not afraid, I am not sure he was convinced. I am not sure I was either! I commanded once more, that in the name of Jesus Christ he was to leave and never return. At that moment I could feel moisture on the top of my head, running down my forehead and cheeks, it must be sweat I thought. Grey Wolf told me to wipe my brow. When I did, I realised that my face and cheeks were bone dry. Grey Wolf was pointing out to me that what I was experiencing from this bad spirit was that he was cashing in on my fear and emotion.

Again I commanded the gentleman to leave the care home, and leave Jane alone to live in peace. All of a sudden there was a foul smell that seemed to be directed into my nose and mouth, as if the smell of death was being breathed upon me (I have no better description). There was a sound of cackled laughter in my head, almost tormenting me. It was hard to keep my concentration but I felt stronger in myself. I called upon Jesus, asking him to be with me, and a voice in my head said to me: "Give a blessing on the room." I started to give my blessing, casting out the darkness, but something was playing with my mind, like chanting in my head, snatching the words I was trying to give in prayer.

I changed the blessing prayer for the Lord's Prayer and started to recite. Within seconds this mind interference was getting worse, making me misquote the prayer. I started all over again, and again came the chanting, it was hard to control. I stopped my prayer and shouted at the spirit causing this confusion. I told him that I would be there all night if need be and that if I were not strong enough to cast him out, then another stronger soul would follow me and maybe another, until he had been banished from this material plane. Once again I started to recite the Lord's Prayer, but my eyes were drawn to the followers of this spirit, only to see that they disappeared. My eyes searched for them throughout the room as I carried on with the prayer, with more vigour. There was a sense of victory, but I knew that I could not let my guard down.

My prayers continued till I felt the room become warmer, the sense of being alone came over me and I felt very emotional. The room had returned to its normal size and light. Once more I gave a prayer, blessing the house and all who dwelt there and I also repeated the Lord's Prayer, and this time with no chanting, no barracking and no interruptions. Was it really over? I could feel normality within me and once again closeness to my guide. I thanked Grey Wolf and all those that had been present in the light that had protected me. I took a few moments to get my breath back. The shaking had gone and I made my way out of the room to faces staring at me with hope in their hearts.

I sat down at the dining table with Jane and the care home owner, and told them that God willing, the negativity had been cast away. Jane began to cry and patted my hand. I then saw a spirit gentleman standing beside her. I described him to Jane and gave her the name of Charlie. She cried more, and acknowledged Charlie was her husband, "but where had he been?" she asked. I was sure she would be having words with him after I had left!

Charlie told me to tell Jane he had always been there and that he had been pushing the care home owner to get help as it was not possible for him to do it himself. He explained, that despite the fact that she had not "felt him", he never left her for a moment. I explained that I could see him standing close behind her with his hands upon her shoulders and she wept, this time with a smile! I mentioned it was time I left and told her she needed to use the room again to put life back into it. I promised Jane that it had to be revitalised, lived in.

One more thing had also to be accomplished, she had to enter the bedroom with me. To experience the difference for herself. It look a lot of persuading. Eventually I mentioned that her husband Charlie would be joining us, and the decision was backed up by the care home owner saying she would join us too. It was agreed. We entered the bedroom and it felt so warm, which was a relief for me. Jane suggested that the room was brighter than usual, "was that possible?" she asked with tears in her eyes

I declined a cup of tea and biscuits as a reward as it was getting late and I had an early start in the morning. Jane gave me a massive hug and a kiss on the cheek as I left. I promised that I would always be there should she need me. The care home owner showed me the way out to my car, thanked me again and mentioned expenses. I declined and left to go home to my bed. I can assure you I never slept a wink! Everything came back to me, the costumes, the temperature drop and the foul smell that seemed to enter my being. But it was over, at least I hoped it was. Of course it was!

I think the whole evening lasted about two hours, with some discussion at the beginning and then some chatting at the end, so the actual rescue probably took about an hour. Afterwards I remembered the words given to me by my guide, "The forces of the light shall always defeat darkness." and I was witness to this that night.

Many months later I saw the care home owner in my

local doctors' surgery where she was collecting prescriptions for her residents. She came over to me and reintroduced herself to me. She informed me that Jane had passed away some seven months after the spirit rescue evening at her home. She said that Jane was a changed lady. Her love for singing had returned, much to the dismay of some of the other residents! Jane apparently mentioned me to others on numerous occasions and the rest of her life was happy and carefree. She often saw her beloved Charlie in the bedroom. She said that he was guarding her.

Jane had passed in her sleep and was found the next day with a beaming smile on her face. The care home owner said that I should be very proud of what I do, and that a life had been changed in front of her own eyes and that she considered it a privilege to have met me. I just gave her a hug and left with a tear in my eyes, head down so no one could see my emotion. I never was very good at accepting compliments, but I accept them now for all the work I do in the world of light, and which have helped me to overcome many of the fears I experienced then and always.

My first spirit rescue had been successful, thanks to those that work with me from beyond the veil. As you may have worked out, this was not like a scene from the movie *The Exorcist*. OK, it got a little scary at the height of the connection, but the souls that sought to control Jane and her life were 'persuaded' to leave this Earthly plane and enter their new life.

Both here and in the world of Spirit as in most confrontations with those who refuse to pass over, fear was the tool that they endeavoured to rule with. Whatever these misguided souls did in their own former lives, the gentleman obviously was a powerful man with loyal followers and he thought he could stay in this world using the power of fear to control others. Fear can only exist if we allow it to.

After confronting these souls, my guide pointed out to me that the followers (ladies in bonnets) had submitted to the holy power that was present within that room during the cleansing blessing, and decided to exit to where the angels of light were ready to escort them to their new levels of existence in the Spirit world. He said that this gave me and him time to deal with the energy confronting me. Eventually with a little authority and persistence, the spirit gentleman let go of this world to face his Maker.

The rescue we believed at this point was completed. No screaming, no fear (OK, a little at the beginning!), and souls that appeared to have been earthbound since the 16th or 17[th]century had moved on.

I am sure that some people have experienced far more energetic rescues, but I can never forget the bruises on Jane, or the fear in her eyes when she explained her experiences. God bless Jane and her husband Charlie for the experience I was confronted with, and for trusting me and those from the Spirit world to come to their aid.

Spirit rescue benefits both the person who has been affected by an Earthbound spirit and the perpetrator of that interference. It thus brings peace for the 'haunted' for want of a better word. Well I had to put that in somewhere didn't I, for those of you who like ghosts!.

Of all the spirit rescues I have done – and I have done about 20 - I think this was the one that affected me the most. Probably it was the physical proof that it provided. There have been a number of other experiences too, but as time has passed, others in my life have been there to assist me in my work. It is comforting for want of a better word, to have a friend or experienced colleague at hand for whatever reason. But also it can mean I may have to watch out for my colleague as well as myself, but generally we watch each other's backs as it were.

Some rescues can be effective in a very short amount of time and be as simple as giving directions to a stranger. Once the Spirit world has illuminated the **exit light** those on the Earth plane see the pathway out of this world, and if they need a little more help, then there will be a loved one or friend present to beckon them further into the light and their new existence.

Working Remotely

Since that first spirit rescue I have done many more, sometimes with my friend Julie. You may well be surprised to know that we don't always do rescues in person but sometimes remotely. So how do I do that?

I can do two things: I can ask first for information as to where the problem is and what is happening there. For example, is the room cold sometimes for no apparent reason? Then I can ask roughly what the house looks like. I might even ask for my client to send me a sketch of the two floors of the house. Once I have all that I will then remotely offer a prayer for the house and ask for guidance from my guides because they can see what I can't. I will ask to be guided through the house, and as I'm guided through the house with my mind and with my spiritual link I might get to a certain corner and I will get a shudder or some knowing feeling, and then I will leave that corner and move on. Then I will go into the other rooms, and check those and maybe I will find another room where something isn't right. Then I will go upstairs.

If there is a problem upstairs as well as downstairs, nine times out of 10 the problem upstairs will be directly above the problem downstairs. So what you have then is a line of energy moving up and moving down. What I can then do is to flood that house in my mind's eye with light from the spiritual world. I can ask my guide to be present and do this with me, and if there are any places where there are restrictions I ask him if he will ask the other spiritual beings that are with us to help us draw that negativity out. These other beings may be angels or archangels or ascended masters. They are all on a higher spiritual energy plane.

Sometimes people just send me a letter with a description of the house, and if I get that then I can forward it to my friend Julie. She works from home and I work from home. I will make a few notes and then we will compare notes. Generally nine times out of 10 we pick up on exactly the same things, because we are both working in the same place with the same energies. So our conclusions are bound to be about the same. Once or twice when I find that things don't quite tally between us there are usually other reasons for that, for example, an extension might have been built onto the house which alters our remote impressions of what we are sensing. If I can't do a spirit rescue remotely then I will say, "I think I have to come out and visit and feel the vibrations in person." And if they are too far away I suggest they find someone closer.

A Curious Occurrence

Most of the time the spirit rescue works out because the spirit itself wants to find peace. Yes, occasionally I do come across awkward or unpleasant spirits. They will try to scare you, because they feel that the house they are in is their house or it was their house and they don't want to move, so they try to get rid of you as the medium. I have one at the moment, and Julie and I are just trying to work out how to deal with it. It is quite an intriguing case.

Everything about the house is perfect while the family is there, but if the boyfriend of the daughter stays there on his own – he sometimes stays when the family are away and looks after the house - all sorts of things happen to him: he feels the bedclothes move as if someone is getting into bed with him. This only happens when he is there on his own; when he's with his girlfriend nothing happens. He also experiences strange things when he is in the room beneath his bedroom. Julie and I have only just started, we don't know who this spirit is, maybe it is somebody who used to live in that bedroom, and who also spent a lot of time in the room below.

I Am Happy Here

It is frequently the case that a spirit that is in a house feels some kind of attachment either to the house itself or to the people who are living there. For example, I might be consulted by the owner of the house and they say that they feel a presence in a certain room, and they are not happy about this. When I connect with the spirit I will ask them what is going on, and the spirit will say, "I'm happy here, this is where I used to live," or they may say, "My family has moved here and this is why I have moved with them." So then what you have to do is say to them, "Look you're not in the right place."

Those in the Spirit world can come back provided it is all done in the proper way. For example, if they are coming back for a specific reason, or they are visiting for a while, that's fine. However, you also have to consider the people who are living in the house. Their welfare and happiness is important too. Even if the spirit is a nice spirit you might not want to have them around, anymore than you might want your best friend's children popping in whenever they feel like it. So if the person or the people in the house want the spirit to leave then we discuss that with them. We want to handle that carefully because the spirit might very well be related to those who are living in the house. Sometimes the family is happy for the spirit to stay as long as they don't make their presence obvious, in which case we explain that to the spirit. A lot of times people will say to me, "Well as long as she doesn't create a problem she can stay, but I don't want her adjusting pictures like she used to when she visited us."

In fact that is exactly what happened with a cousin of mine in Canada where I did another spirit rescue. He said that there was something funny going on in the house. As I tuned into the house I kept picking up the letter M three times, I heard the name Mary. So I said to him, "There is a Mary there but she's not there to hurt you". He said, "Yes I know that, I'm not worried about anything, but she moves things around." When I talked to the lady, she said to me, "Yes I do move things because they're down in the basement and they shouldn't be there." She was moving golf clubs and things like that. My cousin doesn't play golf, so that's why they were in the basement. This lady also kept saying a hundred, a hundred.

Eventually we sorted it all out. This little old lady had lived in the house until she was 100, and she was the grandmother of someone whom my cousin knew. The recurring letter M referred to the three Marys who were connected to the house.

Julie and I had a little word with this lady through Spirit and asked if she could leave quietly, that the family didn't mind her staying, but they didn't want to know of her presence. Things went quiet for a long time, but when my cousin moved a year or so later she started her old tricks again. So Julie and I linked with her again and I think this time she has really moved on.

When people know that there is a spirit in a house, or

they are told that there is, they ask me what is the spirit seeing, "Are they seeing me in the shower, and other intimate places?" I have always been told that there are limits to what they can see. They do understand the need for discretion. In any case, we do have our free will here and we can cut them off. Yes, when you say that spirits are with you all the time people do get worried. On the other hand you will get those negative spirits who will try and break down the barriers between you and them and create problems so that you know they are there, but that is when you bless them and say, "You cannot come in." If they are a real nuisance that is when you call in mediums like myself and Julie.

Chapter 8

Gladiator Man

On many occasions I have felt like a detective having been asked to solve a puzzle. One of the most curious cases I have had to deal with concerned strange things that were happening in a house about a mile away from my home.

One evening I had a phone call which began in the now all-too -familiar way:

"Hello, is that Roy MacKay?"

"Yes."

"Well, I am afraid you are going to think I am mad but I read somewhere that you deal with hauntings, is that right?"

"Yes, I have dealt with quite a few of those, and happily resolved them."

However, in my own mind I felt I was still a novice. The gentleman's name was John. John was a historical advisor for the film *Gladiator*.

John explained what was happening:

"All sorts of strange things are going on in my house. For example, there's a hairdryer that has started to turn itself on without me doing anything at all, and it's not even plugged in. I use the hairdryer to dry varnish some of the things I make for film production companies. It's weird."

He went on, "Then there is the room I use as a workshop, it gets freezing cold even with a fire on, and things suddenly get thrown across the room and the door slams shut. It's getting a bit scary."

He added, "When my friend David comes here I can feel extremely ill and threatened, but this only lasts while he is here, which is really odd. So what do you think? Do you think you could sort this out?"

I said, "I'll come over to your house and see what I can do."

"Can you come and visit on Wednesday next?

"Yes. Have you any idea why this might be happening?"

"Not really."

"OK, see you Wednesday then."

I was pretty intrigued by what was going on. This really fitted into the category of a poltergeist. Poltergeists are spirits, but with a difference. Whereas most spirits are happy to float around and then move on, poltergeist have been around so long that they have become bored and want somebody to acknowledge that they are here. So the way they get you to acknowledge them is by upsetting things. So they move objects around and throw things. Most people think they are here to cause harm, but it is really because they want attention. They are saying I'm still here. I always think of poltergeists as a bit like children that are fed up with being ignored, so they throw a tantrum as well as physical objects.

This was a first for me; spirit rescues I had done – many of them by this time – but poltergeists I hadn't actually experienced or dealt with. Yet I knew I always had Grey Wolf with me and other guides and spiritual helpers. So armed with that knowledge I went ahead.

This was also the first time I had agreed, a little

reluctantly, to take somebody with me. Katrina was my partner at the time, she was conversant with my work and was very interested in the healing I did as well as the spirit connection. At times Katrina and myself would often sit together to improve our knowledge and experience of our spiritual work. We would link with the world of Spirit in the same manner as we would for a private reading, but on these occasions we would do so for the purpose of asking those in the Spirit world for some inspiration to help with the work I do. And any questions that we felt we needed help with in our own personal lives.

Katrina was very interested in this particular case, as I was. When she asked me if she could accompany me on this session, I have to say, alarm bells rang in my head. After all, I was not sure if I would even be able to control the poltergeist and keep myself safe, let alone keep us both safe in a possibly hostile environment. At first I was very hesitant, but Katrina's nature did not let her down on this occasion, she was determined to attend and somehow I agreed.

A few days later we headed to John's home, which took no more than fifteen minutes. I stopped the car outside as I always do on these occasions, composing myself and asking for my spirit guide "Grey Wolf" to be with me and guide me through what I was about to undertake. I also took the opportunity to give Katrina a pep talk, a few do's and don'ts and that in the event of anything going wrong, that she would listen to my instructions and act on them immediately. The do's and don'ts were really to remind her that I was taking charge of the evening and would be responsible for what happened, and that she should not try to be involved in any way, nor even listen to any communication that she might hear from the spirit that we were about to encounter. The reason I said all that to her is because in these circumstances the spirit or poltergeist will do everything they can to distract a medium from their work, because the spirit doesn't want to be moved. They want to continue doing what they have been doing, so they will take any opportunity to confuse or obstruct the medium.

Katrina agreed to a degree. She said, "But if they say nasty things about you I will defend you", so I had to say, "No, please you must not do that, because I want the spirit to give all their attention to me, so I can dialogue with them and release them from the house. That is my job. All I want you to do is to experience it".

So we then made a short prayer together to ask for protection within the environment we were entering, and I opened my psychic centres in order to connect and converse with the spirits that would definitely know we were coming. I gave Katrina a pat on the hand, reminded her of my instructions and away we went.

We knocked on John's door several times before anybody opened it, which seemed strange given that he knew we were coming. Did the poltergeist not want us to come in? I walked in first. In normal circumstances I would always let a lady enter first but these were not normal circumstances, and my natural protective feelings towards my partner kicked in. As I entered the home, there was a strange feeling as if I was walking through a large cobweb, but there was nothing there. Katrina did not mention anything touching her face so I presumed it was for my benefit. I had learned through experience that spirits and poltergeists try many tricks to unnerve us, to give them an edge, to instill a little fear into those entering the domain they are residing in.

I introduced myself to John and heard a whisper in my ear clear as a bell. The words were "fuck off." John began talking to us and again the voice interrupted, "fuck off." Fortunately this wasn't audible to John or Katrina. John explained the goings on, the noises upstairs when he was downstairs and the noises downstairs when at the top of the house.

I asked John, "How well do you sleep at night."

"Generally sound, but I have one hand on the Bible."

John was nervous as he said this, so it made me wonder how well he did in fact sleep.

We noticed the temperature was dropping rapidly as John led us into the living room. Living room! It was not a living room, it was a workshop, and there was even an anvil in front of the fireplace. I couldn't believe what I saw. The walls were adorned with all kinds of Roman shields, each about three feet long. I can remember holding my laughter when he mentioned it was a little untidy! I didn't want to appear rude as he was obviously a very skilled man.

John was very pleasant and explained that his passion was history and that he had been advisor to the movie *Gladiator.* As he continued, I could see the moisture rising on my lips, just like walking outside on a cold frosty morning. I felt a presence to my left hand side and once more I heard the voice say to me, "You are not wanted here, go now." I replied to the poltergeist out loud, "We are not going anywhere, it is you that must leave." I heard him reply with a laugh. So I once again said to him out loud, "This is not your home, your home belongs in the next world, and you have no right to interfere with the material world."

I felt the cold move behind me, it was pretty obvious that the cold was part of this spirit's energy and as I was thinking just that, I felt physical contact with this soul. It was just as if a bony finger was poked into both sides of my lower back. I managed to contain my surprise by holding still. I turned and looked at Katrina but there was no expression of shock or surprise, so I presumed that the attention of this unhappy spirit was fully on me, which is how I hoped it would be.

Katrina, said one or two things to John, but I wasn't aware of what was actually being said as I was trying to keep the attention of our spirit friend. Again there was cold moving around my body, trying to find the fear within me.

I was then - strange as it would seem - distracted by my guide Grey Wolf and his instructions. He told me it would be wise for me to continue my connection to the spirit in the hallway of the house. I acknowledged what he said to me and continued to stand my ground, informing the poltergeist that I was going to help him vacate this world and move into his new world. Once more Grey Wolf interrupted my chain of thought by suggesting that we all move to the hallway and continue the connection with the spirit there.

I didn't at that moment understand why Grey Wolf wanted me to do this. In fact I was about to say to him, thank you, but I am fine here. But without a second's hesitation, Grey Wolf said to me, "You are not listening." Suddenly everything in the room was hushed, I could hear nothing but Grey Wolf's voice, no other conversation, just his voice. He had completely and purposely blocked my hearing in order to get my full attention. Grey Wolf reminded me that I had been told that the poltergeist had the habit of throwing things around when provoked. Grey Wolf continued, "Look around my friend, what do you see?" I must have been in a dream world, because I could not at first relate to what he was showing me.

Then it hit me, not literally, thank God. Grey Wolf was showing me that there were spears leaning against one wall, and on top of the filing cabinets situated around the living room there were knives and swords. In the corner was a mace and chain. Finally the penny dropped! We could have been prime targets for all these weapons that could very shortly become missiles.

As I ushered us all into the hallway and gave my reason

for doing so, I am sure Grey Wolf rolled his eyes up at me. After gaining more information I asked John if he would get me a glass of water as I was going to cleanse the rooms with water and prayer. John obliged. I took the glass of water and blessed it with prayer. I started to bless the living room and felt very nervous with the way the spirit's energies were flipping me around, trying to unnerve me and interfere with my efforts. The prayers were a mixture of commanding the resident spirit to leave the property and to follow the guides from the Spirit world into the light and leave this world behind. We continued with prayers and water to bless all the rooms and doorways, sealing them so the spirit could not return, room by room.

We then proceeded upstairs. I was for a second concerned as I felt there were two attempts to push me downstairs, but these were thwarted by Grey Wolf and the energies of those good spirits who were with me. We entered the bathroom and it looked like a war zone. I asked why there was so much toothpaste on the bathroom cabinet mirror. John explained that he believed it was from his girlfriend who had died some time ago. He believed it was her who had made all the mess, because her name had been written in toothpaste on the mirror.

He didn't want to do anything about the poltergeist because he hoped it was actually *her.* This unfortunately was the poltergeist tricking John to think that was the case, and therefore dissuade him from seeking out a medium who would get the poltergeist to leave the house. The longer that the poltergeist was there the stronger his energies would become and so the stronger his hold on John's home. John admitted that this could not go on - being afraid of every evening's bumps and knocks - and that the situation had got completely out of hand.

The bathroom had to be blessed several times. The

bedrooms were all blessed, I even opened the hatch to the loft and sealed that with holy water. Prayers were said in each room, as far as we could enter them, owing to the vast amount of papers, documents and film props John was storing. John was a great guy and just let us do our work without interruption.

After the evening was brought to a close, we blessed the main entrance, and Katrina and I left. We then sat for a while in the car getting our senses back. I didn't mention any of the spirit's threats to me, and I was thinking to myself, I am glad I did not show fear in front of Katrina as it poked me in my sides. I was quite proud of how I had conducted myself. I gave a prayer and a blessing and cleansing of me and my partner, and prepared to drive home.

However, as I started up the car and waited for the heater to kick in, Katrina said,

"Roy, did you feel anything".

"No, it was fine, why?"

"Well, when we were in the living room it felt like someone was poking their boney fingers deep into my sides, but I didn't want to acknowledge it because you were working and I didn't want to worry you."

"Actually, I felt the same thing but I didn't want to worry *you*, and in any case my mind was more occupied with that spirit."

I don't know if I laughed or went red.

A week later John rang and thanked us. The house was warm, the hairdryer didn't come to life without being plugged in, the coffee no longer disappeared from his cup and no toothpaste signatures were present on the bathroom mirror, although he mentioned that it was a little sad that the poltergeist wasn't his girlfriend. I gave him a name that had been given to me to pass on to him, which I will call Maria. He acknowledged the name was his lady friend, and

I finished the conversation by telling him that the name was passed to him because she wanted to prove that she was still around him. There were no more issues with things being thrown and there were no more issues with his home.

You feel a great deal of satisfaction when you can calm a dwelling and hopefully help a spirit to transition into the Spirit world, so that their journey can also progress. I can only imagine the warm welcome given to the soul returning to their loved ones in the Spirit world. I wonder what excuses they give for being decades late and not only decades but centuries too in some cases!

You might well ask why do some spirits linger on the Earth plane? Why can't they be 'forced' to leave the Earth world? Of course, in many different ways they can be persuaded but they cannot be forced. The Creator gave each and every one of us 'free will.' If an Earthbound spirit chooses to remain within the realms of the Earth world, that is their prerogative. They may feel they have unfinished business or at least they think they do. It may also be a fear or a religious belief that holds them back. All souls are met by loved ones, friends and colleagues, so that they see the world they are transitioning into. They are encouraged to leave the former life behind and lead their spirit into the light.

Those that refuse for whatever reason notice that without their Earthly body, they are restricted in many ways. After all the material body they once possessed has been destroyed by cremation or burial; either way, the spirit has been disconnected from the Earthly cords. The new body they possess is designed for the new world, not the old.

Many times I have been asked, "Is it that simple? Do we have a redesigned body without ailments, without disease? Well the simple answer is yes. I am then asked, "How do you communicate in the world of spirit then?" The answer is through thought transference, which becomes as natural to you as your voice did before you left this material world.

This thought transference occurs not only between the spirits themselves in the world of Spirit but also between the spirits and ourselves. Yet so often we are unaware of this. So acknowledge those in the world of Spirit when they drop into your mind out of the blue. You know when, for no reason, Mum, Dad, Grandma, Grandpa or another relative or friend in the world of Spirit seems to pop into your mind, it's just another way they are connecting with you, uplifting your day, popping in to see what you are doing. Just say to them, "I know you are there." I can assure you they will be very happy.

It is no wonder that people get the wrong end of the stick, when talking about spirits, especially when your first experience of spirits, hauntings and energies may be watching a film or a play about exorcism. Why is there always a demon, why never a lost soul or entity? Why are the lost, never guided from this world by a priest or some spiritual person?

TV and films make their living from drama, accentuating certain myths and stories. Now don't get me wrong, there have also been some very accurate stories which I am sure must have been influenced by those in the world of Spirit. *Ghost* is an awesome film, very true to life, especially helping us to understand that love does not come to an end with that we call 'death.' If life goes on, then love goes on: a new world and extension of your life, loves and all. And this brings me to my next spirit rescue, a very simple one and in fact one of my favourites.

Chapter 9

Waiting For My Husband

Some time later, Julie and I were invited to a bungalow in Hersham, Surrey. We had been contacted by Sarah, who lived in the bungalow with her husband and daughter. Sarah was doing some domestic work for my sister Sandie, and had told her about some of the strange things that she and her family were experiencing at home. There were lots of little things that they noticed such as bumping sounds and knocks on the woodwork which at first Sarah and her family just laughed off as the usual creaks you can get in a house as the temperature rises and falls. So for a while they thought no more about it, because it didn't seem a problem. But that was about to change. The noises began to increase and footsteps had been heard in the hallway and Sarah occasionally noticed a shadow out of the corner of her eye. That is the kind of thing that is noticeable more to children than adults. Adults merely shrug it off as imagination, but when this begins to happen more frequently as it did with Sarah then the person realises that there is some unexplained presence in the house. Sandie heard Sarah's story and suggested that she get in touch with me.

In the kind of work the Julie and I have done you come across all kinds of different spirits much like people here on earth really. Some are nice, some are awkward, some are threatening, some don't really know where they are and some are just quirky. Well, the spirit we were about to meet was one of the quirky ones, and who in her own way was quite endearing, though a little irritating to Sarah and her family.

Julie and I arrived on a lovely summer's evening and were greeted and invited into the home. There were no negative energies, no unwelcoming spirit presence, just a homely feel. We had a few standard questions as to whether there were any smells or cold spots that were abnormal, and Sarah told us about one or two cold places, but we did not pick up anything.

We both asked for a little history on the house, for example, whether Sarah and her husband had made any changes to the structure. Whenever we visit a house where there have been disturbances by a spirit we ask if any walls have been knocked down or new ones put up, because sometimes that can explain some of the noises that the new owners are hearing. I remember saying to someone in another house, "I can see someone coming through a glass door but there is no glass door here," and then the homeowner saying to me "Oh yes, we removed that." In the bungalow we were now in there hadn't been any major changes, so there was nothing untoward there.

It was only when we both began to sense a female influence that we realised that we were on to something. When we mentioned this to Sarah she agreed, "Yes, that's what I feel." We walked around the house and we felt that this lady had shown herself, and again Sarah agreed. "I've seen her in our bedroom sometimes, and that's when I realised that we needed to do something about this." As we entered the bedroom, I was immediately drawn to the area around the French doors which opened out on to the garden, and Julie and I noticed a few short bursts of light outside the doors. I said to Julie, "I think this is where she has been seen,' and then Sarah agreed, "Yes, that is where we have seen her too.'

Now that we knew what we were dealing with we attempted to communicate with this soul whom in our own minds we called Anne. Her energies were right there in the room with us, and I could feel a restriction in my breathing. I was picking up on the past physical symptoms of this spirit lady as we sat on the bed in the room. My lungs ached. I was also sensing pneumonia which I always experienced - in this kind of work - as a piercing pain through the chest and into the back. I told Sarah and Julie what I was feeling.

Julie also had difficulty with her breathing, "I'm feeling a tightness in my chest" she said. We learned that Anne had passed away in that house and in that very room. As I looked up at the French doors I could just make out a small lady, short in stature. I asked her to connect with us. No reply. I continued talking anyway, telling Anne that she no longer lived in this house and she needed to move on. There was a short reply, "I am not going anywhere". Well at least we had a connection! Again I tried to explain that she was interfering with this family's life and it was no longer her home. She again told me she wasn't going anywhere. I pointed out to her that her loved ones would be waiting for her in the light that she could see. She repeated herself, "I'm not going anywhere, I'm not hurting anybody."

She then dropped a bombshell, "I am waiting for my husband." We asked why? "It is nearly time for him to let go, I have to be here for him." I think we all smiled. We told her that she could wait for him in the Spirit world as he no longer lived in this house. Again she said, "I am not going until he is ready." This was nothing if not intriguing.

Then she told us that he was very near to passing and he would meet her at their house, this house. Again we explained it was no longer their home but Sarah's. No matter how hard I tried, she would not listen. She was adamant. In my heart I wanted to leave it at that, I thought about blessing the home, helping her to pass into Spirit with no chance of return at this time, but I just couldn't bring myself to do it, it was my own battle.

Spirits and loved ones are not restricted from visiting those of us they leave behind. But it is necessary for them to take a leap of faith, as we might call it, and connect with the new world, so they have to let go of this plane in order to complete their transition into a full spirit body. Once this transition is complete they have their own choice to a degree as to whom and where they can return to. I have known a spirit to move into the light and return very shortly afterwards to let loved ones know that they have, shall we say relocated, for want of a better word!

Then I saw this spirit lady in my mind's eye, a small lady of slight build, and the impression that she gave me was of a very tired soul who had lost so much weight and energy in leaving the Earthly world. I could not help but think of my Nan when I saw her. This lady continued talking, "He knows this house. He will meet me here. He has no sense of direction, he will never find his way over without me. I had to always help him. I have to be here, he can be so stubborn." We had to laugh at that, as she could only see one stubborn soul, whilst we had two.

I believe at this stage we decided to allow her a little time to see if she would leave of her own accord. Sarah even mentioned that she was not disruptive, and I think that we suggested that we would just let things be for a few days, and see what happened. We had a short chat with Sarah and then left to go to our homes.

That night as I was just about falling asleep I heard a whisper in my ear, a very gentle distinctive "thank you" was whispered. I got the impression that all was at peace and her wait was not in vain. Next day I shared this news with Julie and we were content to know that Anne and her husband had gone into the light together as they had wished. Sarah told us a few days later that the house was now a warmer, happier environment and there had been no more sightings. So long Anne, you won, and we were glad you did. God bless you!

There have been so many lovely rescues throughout our work and very gratifying. So do not believe all that you hear or see on the TV or in films, which is so often scary sensationalism. How many times in those programmes about hauntings is there an attempt to help those spirits who are trapped by helping them out of their predicament and removing what has held them back from entering the next world? And on that note I will next share with you a very different spirit rescue that seemed to be very challenging at the beginning but which eventually turned out well.

Chapter 10

The Laird Of Godalming

Those who have departed this life sometimes continue to take an interest in what happens on the Earth plane at least for a while. They may even return in spirit for short periods, especially if they feel an attachment to a family, or some person, or a group of people, or a place that they have known. They may come back because they want to offer protection or guidance to someone or because they have some emotional concern that draws them back to the physical realm. In some instances it is clear that they have never fully left the Earth plane so great is their attachment. This might be the result of some trauma, or what we would nowadays call unfinished business, or because of some fierce attachment to a particular building. This is usually a house that they have lived in.

The story I am about to tell you is exactly that: it is of a man who felt such love and dedication to his property and who railed against what had happened to its surrounding land that he could not abide anyone else living there. It is a story of frustration, anger and sadness, of someone who wanted to roll back history, but of course could not. So he was stuck literally in a time warp. And in doing so he made life pretty uncomfortable for others, which happily Julie and I were able to redress, and at the same time we helped him to enter the next world where he could recreate the land he wanted and care for.

One evening, I received an anxious call from a lady asking for our help for her brother, who lived in a village high above the town of Godalming in Surrey about four miles south of Guildford. Godalming is set in a valley with wooded hills all around amongst which are several ancient villages. Godalming itself has a long history lying as it does on the old stagecoach road to Portsmouth.

This lady, whom I think was called Carol, told us that she feared for her brother Colin's sanity as he had been experiencing so much paranormal activity in his home, some of which sounded quite extreme. This had been going on for ages and Colin and his sister couldn't find anyone willing to help. So she turned to us hoping that we could do so. She had heard about some of the work we had taken on in the past and asked us if we would consider meeting her brother Colin at his home. She explained to me some of the things that had been happening: freezing temperatures in his bedroom when outside the temperature was ambient; a light emanating from a mirror in the room; bedclothes shifting; something moving about the room; and muffled noises. The light from the mirror was so annoying that eventually her brother had moved it to another room. This all sounded very curious and I offered to help. I thought it would be a good idea to bring Katrina again, who had accompanied me on the 'Gladiator' rescue, and whom I had been helping develop the gifts of mediumship and psychic ability. It would be not so much of a test, but more an experience for her. I also brought Julie again.

Julie had become a close friend over the years and had helped me with several successful spirit rescues including remote rescues, (cleansing homes without the necessity of visiting the property in question). With experience one can project energies across the world to their necessary destination. Think of when you send a prayer for a loved one who is in need. Well it's the same principle when dealing with spirits.

Julie had shown herself to be a valuable asset in the procedures we had performed in the past some of which I have already referred to. She is not easily spooked by the antics of odd spirit activity and poltergeist shenanigans. This is vital when you are in a delicate situation and you need someone to 'watch your back.' Her Welsh heritage shows in her tenacity to get things right whilst under pressure. When you are working with a colleague in these circumstances there needs to be an unspoken understanding between you that some comments and commands shouldn't be questioned, so that if one of you shouts jump, the other one jumps because in some extreme cases your safety could depend on it. That kind of understanding is one that Julie and I have with each other. Needless to say Julie accepted this assignment without hesitation.

With Katrina and Julie on board I made arrangements to visit Colin and his house one evening as soon as possible, which he much appreciated. I picked up Julie who lived close by and then drove eight or nine miles to Guildford to collect Katrina, and then on towards Godalming just three miles south. We arrived outside the house early evening. Seated in the car nearby we gave a short prayer and a short meditation, asking for our guides that work with us to be present with us for the duration of the visit, and of course for protection from unseen forces that might be present in the house.

When we enter a situation such as this we are all aware of the individual responsibility before us and of the need to protect the 'crew' as we call ourselves. We will all have different interpretations of our experiences according to our own capabilities, which simply means that each of us is likely to sense or see things slightly differently from our colleagues. So at any one moment I might notice something more strongly or less strongly than the others, and similarly they might remark upon something before I do. So in this way we are all supporting each other and creating a fuller understanding of what we are experiencing in our own way.

We knocked on the front door and Colin introduced himself, thanking us profusely for agreeing to help in whatever way we could. We then entered the house, or perhaps I should say the house entered us because as soon as we crossed the threshold the cold entered our bodies. In most people's houses you feel warm as you enter, but with this house it was the cold that welcomed you, and that was just the beginning. What I also felt straightaway was a restriction in my breathing. As a child I suffered with asthma as I mentioned in an earlier chapter, and I am always very cautious when the air quality is different from normal. To Julie and Katrina the air seemed normal but to me it was piercingly cold. I felt hoarse inside.

Colin led us up the stairs immediately in front of us to the landing above, and before we reached the landing he turned and informed us that we would feel the temperature change further. I recall that we were halted at the top of the stairs for a moment while Colin told us what to expect. Standing at the top of the stairs I felt we were in a very precarious position, so I pushed myself up the stairs and onto the landing and beckoned the others to follow me. It's much safer to forestall any dangerous situations before they happen, and it would not have been the first time that I have had a troublesome spirit try to push me down a staircase. While I had come up the stairs I had had that cobweby feeling on my face, which is spirits touching you, and I also felt the energy of the spirit that was causing so much disturbance. Julie, for her part, said that there was something not quite right with the front room downstairs.

On the landing Colin began to tell us of the frightening abnormalities that he was experiencing in his home which he was sharing with us anxiously. There were a whole catalogue of things:

"I hear voices in the middle of the night while I'm in bed, and it's the same when my partner is here too. In fact when she is here we can feel hands on our shoulders when we are cuddling up close together at very intimate moments."

He went on, "I think the worst thing is the freezing cold temperatures In the room even in the summer months, and some mornings it's not just the cold but a freezing mist rising halfway up the bedroom walls like the sort of mist you see in the country on a very frosty morning. Sometimes I wake up at two o'clock in the morning and the mist is already there."

But there was more to his tale: "Then there are the times when we feel the bedclothes being moved away as if someone is trying to wake us up, when all we want to do is get closer together to try and be warm. The other thing is hearing all sorts of odd noises, as if someone is walking in and out of the bathroom, moving things, picking things up, that sort of thing."

Colin also told us about the mirror that had flickering light coming through it, which he had to remove to another room and cover up, as he was always being drawn to it expecting to see something or someone in the reflections.

He also talked about seeing something like a shadow moving around the bedroom, and at one stage he said he thought he was seeing little spikey black balls spinning in the room. No wonder at one point he thought he might be going mad, and his sister feared for his sanity.

So before I continue, and tell you how we dealt with this, what was going on here? What you have to remember is that when you have a really troublesome spirit or spirits, they are working on your fears. To get their way they are working on the fear element in you. So they will show you all sorts of things, things with red eyes, things crawling around and other nasties, because they want to scare you, because they don't want you around. They want to be in charge. What we say to people who struggle against things like this is, "You have to say to yourself, try and imagine these alien things like a B movie or a horror movie. You have to laugh, so you laugh at what you are seeing, and that gives you your strength, and also it demeans them rather than them demeaning you."

What you always need to do in these situations is to make it plain that it is you who is in charge, and in the name of God it is they who need to go. Remember how I dealt with that man and his two female followers who were making life a misery for that poor little old lady in that care home.? I stood my ground and used the power of the Light to send them away. I always remember what my guide once said to me: "In a room filled with light you don't notice a spot of darkness, but in a room filled with darkness you will always see a spot of light. That is why the forces of light are so much more powerful than the forces of darkness."

So back to my story. Colin guided us into the offending bedroom and the cold was obvious, and once again my breathing was taking a bashing. In front of us was the bed, to our left was a large window, ahead of us beyond the bed was a wardrobe and in the far right hand corner was a cupboard. We stood still and allowed our senses to open up. This was to allow us to communicate through many different channels until we could sense the problems and the spirits that were present. I asked Julie and Katrina for their impressions and as expected we all gave different findings.

Once more we continued to search the energies and in doing so I was drawn to the small cupboard in the far right of the room. I shared my findings and made my way around the bed in front of us to the cupboard in question, the energies were very strong in that area and the temperature dropped. There was a sudden feeling that we were being observed and not by each other. I openly tried to connect with the energy and the residual spirit several times but without a link of any sort.

Julie informed me that from her view, the small cupboard was bulging as if a cartoon character was trying to fight its way out of a room. I wasn't sensing this, though as I explained earlier we all tune in on different levels. I offered a prayer and a blessing to that area of the room, and as I did so I could suddenly see movement in the door just as Julie had described. I moved backwards to the end of the bed and continued trying to connect with the spirits present. I gave another prayer and suddenly I was picking up on energies just a few feet away. I could feel negative energy moving toward me. I spoke up openly, calling on the spirits within this property to make themselves known to us. I coughed as again my breathing was being affected. I looked across to Julie and Katrina who seemed quite calm, so I could ascertain from this that they were not affected.

I continued talking out aloud to the spirit, asking that we may have the privilege to connect with them. I informed them that the home was no longer theirs, that it had new owners, owners that deserved to be left to live in peace. There was a clear sound of someone clearing their throat. Then I heard a spirit communicating with me at last. The voice said to me, "I beg your pardon sir, it is you that do not belong here, It is my property and thus I would ask you to leave immediately".

We had a few seconds of quiet and I began to feel this spirit presenting itself to me, and as I started to receive visual energies around me I looked at Julie and Katrina. Julie was concentrating with her eyes closed. "We have a gentleman here" I said to Colin, "I pick up that he is of a good height too", Colin nodded. The spirit in question made itself more and more available to our psychic sight. The very first thought as I saw him was the image of Abraham Lincoln. Between Julie and myself we began to describe the soul. I said, "He has a very smart dark suit on here with a white shirt, he is leaning on a walking stick with his left hand and the handle looks metallic, silver possibly." Julie commented, "His cheeks seem chubby and his sideburns seem to draw attention to his face." Then I commented on his big black hat, and before I finished Julie said, "His hat is like a top hat only taller." She had taken the words right out of my mouth, it looked like a stove pipe hat. (Funnily enough there is a photo of Lincoln wearing such a hat, not that I am suggesting for a moment that the spirit was Abraham Lincoln, but if you see the photo online you will get a feel for what we were seeing).

Clearly this spirit was noticeable to us both now. And Colin acknowledged that he could relate to our descriptions. The gentleman snorted, "Once again, this is my property sir, and I must ask you to leave." Then strangely as time passed this man became calmer and the room warmed a little. I repeated that this was not his property, it had been sold several times over since he was the owner. This obviously annoyed him as he began stamping the cane on the floor again to emphasise his anger. I continued to explain that his time upon this Earth was over and that he had a new world waiting for him.

Once more he raised his voice, but this time the message was different, "Have you seen what they have done to my land"? Have you? It has been raped Sir! This was a most beautiful part of the country, it's a pit of its former self." As he said this I was seeing excavating diggers digging out stone. (Only recently have I learnt that the hills around Godalming have long been excavated for their special Bargate stone, which has been used over the centuries for building churches and other public buildings. This quarrying for stone no doubt increased after the railway line arrived at Godalming in 1859, and that would probably explain what this spirit meant by the "rape" of his land). I now felt this man moving towards me, but it was no longer the anger that I felt but a sadness for what had been lost.

Artist's impression of the Laird

We continued to explain that he would have land in his new world, the world in which his family has passed into many decades before, a land that nobody would be able to take from him. We continued to try and persuade the spirit of this man to vacate this world. Several times he banged his cane on the floor. I was beginning to sense his sadness even more now, a sadness that was inevitably starting to touch my inner self as it brought a tear to my eye.

Then something very unexpected and marvelous happened. Just as I took a deep breath to continue, suddenly everything seemed to become silent. The silence was broken by Julie's voice. She explained to us that she had a spirit lady and a child standing right next to her. These were clearly spirit people. Julie felt that the younger girl was the daughter of the older spirit lady, who herself appeared to be of no great age. For a moment it seemed that the room had become very still and a warmth was evident. The gentleman we had been talking to had become very still and seemed mesmerised as he stared in the direction of the spirit females that had joined us. It was clear to us now that the spirit ladies had come forward to aid in the transition of the top hatted gentleman. We could not ascertain whether these ladies were his family or kin, but the energies they brought with them were welcoming, gentle and warming. Then before our eyes the ladies drifted away out of our human sight, the top hatted gent was still gazing in Julie's direction, and then he too drifted away. Peace at last.

I think there was a great feeling of relief all around, and we dared to presume that he had finally passed to the world of Spirit aided by the lovely spirit ladies. I was sure that in his time he was a man of substance, and from his manner with me although polite, he did not take kindly to being pushed in any way whatsoever. But he left peace in his wake and that's all that mattered to us. Was he really a laird? We shall never know, but I did feel a Scottish connection somewhere. He certainly felt like a laird.

We left the bedroom with respect for the departed spirits that had been with us. Then we discussed the points of the rescue on the landing with Colin and his sister before making our way downstairs to our car parked nearby. Once we were sitting comfortably in the car we gave thanks in prayer and took a few moments to relax and congratulate each other on a job well done. We didn't linger very long because I was anxious to get home quickly as I was leaving to go to Canada in the next couple of days and still had lots to pack and lots of things to do before I could leave for my flight.

However on the day I was due to leave for Heathrow I was contacted once again by Colin. He acknowledged that the home was "so different now" and he was very grateful for that, but there was a new problem. He explained, "You will probably think I am going insane, but I've been seeing 'things' scurrying around the house. They look like little demons, that sort of thing." I explained that he was not going mad. However, I was not in a position to return to his home because I was literally about to leave for Canada very shortly and I would be away for weeks.

So again I called on Julie to start remote cleansing on Colin's home. This would be more effective than it might seem because having visited the home we were familiar with the layout of the building. Julie agreed and I told her that I would also connect with her after I had settled in Canada. The visit to Canada had been a long time in the planning and was very important to me as it was the home of my father's family, and their friends.

Julie worked hard on sweeping or cleansing Colin's home remotely whilst I was away, and she admitted catching sight of several malevolent spirits and mischievous souls that had hidden away within the energies of the home. I helped where I could linking in from Canada when I had time to do so.

Julie told me that she had not had any feedback from Colin, so after a short while we presumed all was well within his property. Feedback is vital in these circumstances because otherwise all our good work can be undone, especially where malevolent beings are concerned.

Now, you might well ask why didn't we pick up on these other negative energies?

The answer is that such negative energies can hide. They can disappear from your radar.

When I got back to Britain some weeks later we had some more news about Colin's house. Apparently there were still problems with his 'demons,' and he asked us to return and help. Colin also admitted that during the period when the remote clearance was being undertaken he had hired a couple who told him they could rid the home of bad spirits, and that they had entered the house to exorcise them. Colin told us that they entered the main bedroom on their own, not allowing anyone else to join them. That is something that I will not do because of obvious security reasons. In any case I always think it is more respectful for the occupant of a room to be with me when I enter it.

Colin told us that the couple looked into the bedroom, spent a short while there, came out and charged £200, and that when he asked them for their findings they became very cagey. They also told him that if he wanted to get the house totally cleared, he would need to put Jesus into his heart. This was how the visit was described to us. It is not my place to judge.

Soon after Colin's phone call Julie and I returned to his house. We set about cleansing and securing the home with prayer and by sealing the doors and windows with holy water, thus denying any more negativity from entering the home. While I was working Julie had picked up that an elderly lady was happily sitting in a rocking chair smiling. Julie was able to describe the lady so perfectly that Colin's sister who was with us at the time, could recognise the soul as the elderly lady that had lived and passed away in a downstairs room. She looked so content, before disappearing from view.

Once again the home was secure from paranormal activity. Colin wrote a lovely letter to us afterwards:

"I would like to thank you and Katrina and Julie for removing a spirit that was in our house for so many years. Without your help we would still be suffering the noises, the moving about in the night and the sleepless nights. I was a non-believer in this sort of thing, but once it happens to you life after death becomes a reality. You never gave up on us. Right from the beginning you were with us. We thought we were going a bit mad until we contacted you and your team. I believe what you have is a gift, and I hope you continue forever, because without you people I don't know what we would have done. The house now is completely different. It's peaceful, as before it was so scary." Well thank you for that, Colin. We were glad to be of help.

Chapter 11

I Can't Win Them All

When you are working with the world of Spirit you cannot take things for granted. This is especially the case when those on the Earth plane interfere with or interrupt what you are trying to do. My next story illustrates what I mean.

Some years ago I received a call from a lady living near Dorking in Surrey. She told me that there were disturbing things happening in her home: objects being moved around the house, lots of bumps and noises in the middle of the night together with the sound of footsteps up and down the stairs. She said, "We've tried very hard to come to terms with these things, but we have reached a point where we feel we can no longer live with these disturbances." (She was living there with her husband and young daughter.)

She then explained, "We're living in a very old cottage that goes back to about the 16th century, so it has lots of history. Sometimes we feel that we are 'sharing' our home with some of the people who lived here before us a long time ago. Maybe one or two of the previous owners are causing these things. But it is more than that, because recently our young daughter has been waking up in the middle of the night screaming, and she says that sometimes she sees somebody staring at her as she wakes up." The lady added that hearing bumps and creaks in the night was one thing, but having a child upset was quite another matter which the family was not prepared to put up with. I agreed wholeheartedly with that.

As the lady gave me a little more information, my guide automatically linked with me saying there had been some upheaval in the home. When I hear that word from my guide it usually means that there has been some physical upheaval like walls being knocked down or doors being moved or replaced. So I asked if there had been any other problems going on apart from the spirit visitors, and the lady said no at first, but then said, "Well, we are having some renovations and changes made to the house if that's relevant." It certainly was if my guide was bringing the subject up.

There are many instances when physical changes to a home cause a negative reaction from those spirits that had a connection with the home in previous times. People who have passed over often keep a protective eye on a house which they once loved or owned. Yes it may sound a bit silly, but just as there are those on the Earth that don't like change to what they have become accustomed to, so there are also those in the world of Spirit that get attached to the home they loved, and they want to see it stay as it was. After all, remember the Laird of Godalming; he was attached to his old house and to the land surrounding it.

As always I offered to work remotely with my colleague Julie, but the lady said she would prefer me to come to the house and she would appreciate me coming as soon as possible. We arranged a time for two days later, which was the earliest I could manage as I was busy with other work.

However, in between it gave Julie and I the opportunity to work remotely with the old cottage and gain some insight as to what was happening there. I gave Julie some information but not everything, because as always I did not want to interfere with any information she could gain from her own psychic investigations.

On the day in question I arrived at the lovely property and sat outside composing myself admiring the idyllic scene. The cottage looked just like what you used to see on the lid of those very big chocolate boxes that confectioners used to sell, with roses curling around the walls and wisps of laburnum and lilac around the door, the sort of cottage you might see in children's fairy stories. I went to open the front gate but it was so stiff I decided to enter by the side gate. I then stood back for a moment to admire the tiny window panes, and my eyes were drawn to a window on the far right of the cottage and straight into the eyes of a middle aged lady who was peering down at me. She was in grey as far as I could remember apart from a white bonnet or cap, I stared for a few moments quite amazed. I don't always see a spirit form so clearly. From what she was wearing I could see that she was a spirit from centuries past. I blinked and she was gone. It requires a lot of psychic energy for a spirit to manifest themselves so clearly in that way, which is why I rarely see something like that.

I knocked on the old oak door. It wasn't huge but it was mighty heavy and it made such a clanking sound that you would have thought the cottage was a hollow vessel. I half expected to see a large butler dressed in black open the door and beckon me to come in. However I was pleasantly surprised when a lady with a beaming smile popped her head around from the heavy door enquiring, "Are you Roy"? As she opened the door to bid me enter I could hear a scuffle of feet running on the wooden floorboards. I looked for children, but I could only see one pretty young girl about four years old at a guess and the only child in view.

The cottage with its low ceilings and strong beams was so pretty inside, though light was restricted a little as you would expect of an aged property with small windows. The lady introduced me to the young girl who was quite talkative. "She is not at play school today as she hasn't been well," she commented. As she closed the door behind us, I said how fabulous the old heavy door was and enquired as to its age. I was amazed to learn that it had once stood in Hampton Court Palace in the reign of King Henry V111. So it was nearly 500 years old! Wow, what about that for history.

The owner of the property was talking about her daughter's ill health, which I believe was mumps, but I could be wrong. What I remember was that I hoped it was something that I had already had as a child and not something I could pick up.

I very quickly steered the conversation around to the problems with the house, and as with her conversation on the phone to me, she repeated pretty much the same description again. I asked if there were other children in the house, and she told me there were not. I informed her that I had heard the scurrying of tiny feet as I entered her property, "Ahh" she said "I will tell you about that later".

I also recalled that Julie (working remotely) had earlier picked up children running around, especially in the vicinity of the stairs, which was exactly what I was sensing. The lady invited me to look around the home, which gave me the opportunity to bring up 'the lady at the window' as I shall call her. I described that lady as I had seen her and the fact that she was looking out as if she was waiting for somebody to arrive. I had by this time presumed that 'the lady at the window' was not looking at me as I first thought. The lady of the house found the sighting very interesting.

I continued through the house into the small kitchen, and as I was admiring the view to the garden I felt someone bump into the side of me as if brushing past or around me. I expected to see the daughter as I looked down, but she was still in the arms of her mother.

I asked if anyone had experienced anything unusual in the kitchen, and she asked me, "What sort of experience?". So I explained what had just happened to me in the kitchen. "Oh I always feel that someone is with me when I enter here. I get like the feeling of a draught whipping around me and this room never really warms up". By now, I was feeling lots of different vibrations, and I explained that I could confirm Julie's finding that there were children around the house and that I could now sense them too. The lady then showed me into her husband's den or office. I cannot recall meeting him at this stage but I could be wrong. Certainly on this occasion the lady of the house was giving me all the information and the tour of the home.

I asked if we could make our way upstairs, and she agreed and offered me the opportunity to go first which I did. As I walked up the stairs I had a strange feeling, as if I was passing people on the stairs, you know, people trying to shuffle past. However this was not the case as the stairwell was empty apart from me and my tour guide ascending behind me. As we got to the top I could feel a change of energy and also temperature. It was decidedly cooler. I commented on this but the house owner almost shrugged it off. I was feeling that she was not going to enlighten me until I had finished with my inspection.

I could see that there was obviously building work going on and that walls were being changed or renovated. Old style plaster was clearly visible, in fact it was quite fascinating, one or two areas were half wall and half studding, The parents' bed and the daughter's bed were in two separate rooms, but with the walls being renovated each could see the other whilst in bed.

I made my way into the daughter's rooms, and once again the vibration changed, and I saw someone brushing past me. I could see it was a thin looking gentleman with a long coat. I also suddenly felt that my movements were being monitored. While all this was going on I could sense that my own persona was being buffeted around by the energies I was experiencing. I was also sensing someone with a strong air of authority in front of the bedroom window, followed by a sequence of moving shadows. I knew I was picking up a male vibration. I spoke out aloud so as to connect with the spirit or spirits present. It remained silent as I stepped further into the room. Then something totally unexpected happened; as I turned round to talk to the lady of the house the room behind me completely changed. I saw a blackboard with writing on it with what looked like addition and subtraction tables, and I could see a cane or pointed stick leaning against the bottom half of the blackboard. There were books on the floor around the base of the easel and the room felt cluttered. These visuals only lasted a few moments. I heard a bell very clearly even though it was slightly muffled as if someone had their hand inside muffling the clapper, (the part that strikes the inside of the bell). So that told me that the room had once been used as a classroom.

There were noises on the landing and the stairs, and I asked the lady if she had experienced the sound of people rushing around upstairs and she acknowledged that she had. I told her that I was feeling as if I was in a school and explained what I had seen.

She said that at one time the cottage had indeed been a school. That supported everything I was experiencing, but I felt that this had not been a conventional school where children attend from outside, but that they had actually lived there with their tutors as it were. I explained this as well, adding that this had been a school under very strict supervision and that the children went to bed in the dark and awoke in the dark. I could sense the scene as covers were pulled off the beds to force the overtired children to rise for prayers etc.

The lady of the house said to me that on a number of occasions she had been woken around 5 a.m. and that the duvet was pulled completely off their bed. So although this didn't happen every night it was happening from time to time, which was annoying. She said that on one occasion she pulled the duvet back in mid-flow, only to have the duvet pulled right off the bed and onto the floor. She also mentioned that there had been times when she had sworn out aloud to whatever was doing this, after which it would be a while before it reoccurred.

I spoke out aloud to the figure I could sense around me. I told them that it was not acceptable that he or they were continuing to occupy the home which no longer belonged to them and that they were commanded to move into the world of Spirit. I received no reply. So once more I gave a prayer and a blessing to the upstairs of the house. Calling on the powers of God to assist me in this transition, I went to the windows where I had sensed the gentleman standing there which was also the same window that the lady in the grey dress and white cap had been looking out from.

Reciting a prayer, after ushering the spirits out through the window, I asked that the windows be sealed by the protection of the Spirit world and that nothing other than positivity and protection would be allowed to enter and remain. I proceeded to bless and seal with prayer the other windows on this floor level. As I was blessing the window at the rear of the house I heard a voice that seemed to be directly behind me: "It's not right" the voice said "damaging this property." I tried to connect with the voice but it seemed to have moved away. So once more I said out aloud that the home now belonged to the family that was inhabiting it and that the house was being improved. Once again I said that those within the house from years before needed to move towards the light and transition into a better world, to be with their families that had moved over before them, and that they cannot stay trying to dominate the lives of those now living in the cottage. I asked that they go in peace, to the rest that they deserve. All the way through this I was explaining to the lady of the house what I was seeing and saying. I blessed all around the child's bed and blessed the area around it repeating my prayers.

The house upstairs was now feeling warmer, and after a short chat we made our way downstairs to repeat the ceremonies. When the temperature warms up afterwards on these occasions it is usually a good sign that the offending spirits have gone and the house can settle and be at peace. After a long chat with the lady of the house I gave her a few things to say and do should the problem continue. I felt reasonably happy that all was well now. On the other hand I hadn't been able to make a direct connection with the spirit that was in the home, which normally happens when I do a spirit rescue, so on this occasion I didn't quite get that feeling of completion, though I was feeling happy that we were at least getting there.

As always I asked the client to keep me up-to-date with anything that was happening afterwards. This allows me to continue sending spiritual energy all the time that I feel it is needed to clear the home. I returned to my car and on the way out I briefly stopped hoping to see another glimpse of that 'lady in the window.' I did not see her. Maybe this was a sign that my job was done.

After a couple of days I received a call from the cottage. The lady of the house said that It was generally quiet apart from one or two incidents. I naturally hoped this was the end to all the problems in the cottage and that our spirit friends had left, but this was not to be.

About another week after my visit I received a call from the lady of the house saying that her daughter was again waking up crying. So I made arrangements to return to the cottage as soon as I could. It is very rare that I get called back in these circumstances, but it was clear that I needed to return.

I returned within a day or two and had a long chat with the lady of the house. She was kind enough to admit that some things had improved, but there was still the feeling of being watched, especially when the family had gone to bed. As we talked I was trying to get the 'feel' of the place again and I remembered my first visit and the sounds of children scampering around the wooden floor. We continued chatting as we made our way into the kitchen area where I had felt somebody brush past me, again it was probably a child. It was still cold in there but no other vibrations were picked up on as previously.

We made our way upstairs and the temperature got a little chilly. It felt as if someone had just opened a window to let in a draught of cold air. I asked if the upper part of the house was always cold. To my surprise the lady said, "No it's lovely and cosy when the heating is on. It's on now." I accepted that it was only me experiencing the change in temperature.

As we reached the top of the stairs I could see that even more restructuring of the cottage had taken place since my last visit. I saw one big open plan bedroom in front of me, because now some walls had been removed and others were work-in-progress.

My first thoughts were of the thin, stern gentleman whom I had seen and felt on my first visit when he had brushed past me. This time I was not picking this up at all, it may just have been that he was avoiding contact with us. After all, he didn't exactly hang around the first time I saw him.

I worked on opening my chakras or psychic centres so I could get a better account of what was happening, tuning to a higher level you might say. As I did this I had a coughing fit which I am pretty sure did not belong to me, my heart started to race and I was not sure whether I was going into trance at that very moment. I gave a quick quiet prayer and asked my guide for an explanation of my feelings. I continued to feel hot and unwell so I decided to close myself off from the vibrations to control these issues.

I did not mention these feelings to the lady of the house as I didn't feel it was necessary or sensible to worry her with what I was experiencing. My primary task was to clear the home of unwanted energies. It was clear that we had a real mix of spirit energies in this home that had seen several centuries of inhabitants. I asked if it was OK to bless the upstairs bedrooms again because I felt I was tuning into several different spirit levels. I then set about my work first blessing the main windows. If you can imagine, I was trying to send the spirit visitors out of the property and blessing all the doorways and windows to prevent their return. I was basically shutting and locking the exits and entrances to the upstairs quarters with blessings and prayers. Once more whilst crossing the open plan bedrooms towards the rear window I experienced another coughing fit, and once more that feeling of gloom and sadness. Again I asked for God to clear the premises from this negativity.

I did feel for a moment that I was working blind as I generally pick up quite a lot of information when doing this work. I blessed the rear window and turned back to face the room, and for the briefest of moments I had the following scene in front of me: there was not just one bed in the bedroom but several - wooden cots some people would call them. They were pretty coarsely made and in a line. There was a waxy smell I recall like camphor or carbolic soap, and I felt it was irritating my breathing and probably was causing my painful cough.

The scene soon faded and I said a prayer to cleanse the room. I asked the lady of the house if she was aware of the history of her property. She said she knew a little. I particularly asked if the cottage had once been some kind hospital or a home for the sick. I recall her saying she could not be 100% sure but she believed there had been in some way, and then added that her home had seen so much history given its age. Yes it was an obvious answer and I wished I hadn't asked the question.

After spending some time discussing things I asked her how she felt at this moment upstairs and she replied, "Quite relaxed really. "As we finished our chat I gave the Lord's Prayer and asked that Archangel Michael would bring new energies to the home. I thanked the lovely lady of the house for her patience during the blessings etc. She was very appreciative and patient. I asked her if she would give me feedback every few days so that I could monitor the situation and work remotely from home through prayer.

I received several positive feedbacks from her and all seemed well. I felt we were dealing with multilevel spirit vibrations and residual energies (energies that keep recurring, sometimes called hauntings) and hoped that the problems had ended.

Unfortunately after a few weeks the daughter started waking up in the middle of the night again upset and crying. Upon hearing this I suggested we continue clearing the vibrations until all was cleansed. However, the lady said she had to inform me that her husband had asked for a priest to come and assist with the problem. I replied that of course that was their prerogative and thanked her for allowing me to play my part in clearing the situation. She thanked me once more and hoped that they would see me again as she had found the work we had performed fascinating. She also thanked me for one or two personal messages that were given to her from her loved ones in the world of Spirit.

It was obvious that she would have liked me to return and complete the spirit rescue, or maybe I should say spirits rescue as there were clearly several, but her husband took a different view. On reflection my hunch is that he wasn't happy for his wife to know what had happened in the cottage in previous centuries. What he also probably did not realise is that when you have such an old building the number of spirits hanging around can be such that the problem cannot always be solved in just one visit or even two.

I prayed for the next few weeks that the problem would soon be resolved. I knew that God and those that work with me in these circumstances have their own way of doing things, and I believe that this was a learning curve for me.

Looking back on those years I learnt about tiered levels of spirit activity and residual energies. I am not saying that those energies were bad or even mischievous. As light workers or empaths we are affected by residual energies, and in my case in the cottage I experienced negative energy, a feeling of nausea and pressure on my chest and coughing fits. I was also picking up the gloom and fear of those poor children. Thankfully, as far as I knew, the family did not experience anything like that.

If a home has been impregnated by anguish or pain it can leave that dark and cold feeling for a long time and change the ambience of a room or a whole building. Many of us are empaths, we sense so many levels of energies.

But remember that residual energies can also be positive. When a house has been happy, vibrant and full of love it can feel like it is full of happiness all the time. You often feel upon entering the homes of others that it has that wonderful homely and loving vibration, and maybe you comment on it. So make your home a home full of laughter and energy, fill it with love and it will repay you with times of peace and relaxation.

I have met so many lovely people in my spirit rescue work, and I have been fortunate to carry on this work for years after this particular cleansing, rescue and blessing. Except for this one incident all my rescue work has met with great success. So what should I think, that for whatever God's reason this one was taken out of my hands? You can't win them all!

Chapter 12

Spiritually Cleansing
Your Home

If you feel you have an unpleasant spirit energy in your home can you cleanse this yourself, or do you have to call in a medium, or some other person who is psychically and spiritually adept at such things? This is a question that has been asked of me and my fellow mediums a number of times over the years, and the advice that we have given is that a lot of success has been experienced by those that have tried our recipe of self-help. So If you should have the need to cleanse your home of a spirit presence, then you may be helped by the following procedures. But first of all, how do you know that you have a 'presence'?

Some people are aware of little knocks and bumps in their residences. After all, our homes are full of water pipes, clocks, electrical appliances etc, all having their own quirks and ways. We know that central heating can cause wooden floors to creak and expand, and when that happens it doesn't generally worry us, because we understand what is going on. It's more unnerving when those stairs and floorboards sound as if somebody is actually walking around or up or down the staircase or from one side of the room to the other. Items that move on a shelf when there is nothing around to shake them and cold spots in rooms are also signs of spirit energies. Many people simply ignore these sounds and sights. Any of these incidents that you feel give you the shudders are not a sign that you have a 'bad spirit' by any means. After all your loved ones from the world of Spirit visit you from time to time, and when you understand this, then for most of us, that becomes acceptable.

But not knowing the source unfortunately makes us uncomfortable and fear breeds fear. Did you know that we share our homes and possessions with the Spirit world all the time? Many spirits pass through our homes, throughout our life; they cannot see you just as you cannot see them. Why? Because they are on a different level of existence. Think of an apartment block: you live on one level and others live above and below you, living their lives not knowing what is happening in your life, and likewise you not knowing about them. You may only be aware of them when they make the odd noise such as when they open a squeaky door, or you might just hear a hello as two neighbours meet. So similarly in the spirit world there are many levels of existence. I suppose you could say it is a world within a world.

Okay, so you feel uneasy for a number of reasons in your own home, noises are increasing, you seem to get the shivers a lot, literally. Shivers are a classic sign of the existence of energies, but don't think they are always negative energies. So here are the remedies that we suggest:

1) The use of prayer to bless and protect your home and occupants is always powerful, and I think a lot of people instinctively recognise that. Just think of

all those houses you have entered where you saw a picture with the words '*bless this house,*' as you walked in through the front door. The power of prayer is very effective in any form of blessing; this can be offered up from one room whilst mentioning the other rooms in the home that you wish blessed. Alternatively you may wish to do each room in turn. Ask in prayer that the Creator cleanse your home with the light and love of the Archangel Michael, warding off any negative energies that should not be present in your home, and allowing positive energies to stay that are necessary for your journey through this life.

2) You may wish to use holy or blessed water to assist you in your prayer, flicking drops of water around door frames, windows and rooms. So how do you get holy water? The easiest way is to add some pure salt or rock salt to a glass of water, and in prayer ask for the water to be blessed. You can even bless the water yourself with a prayer, lots of people bless their food and drink every mealtime, and didn't you ever say grace before a meal? You are giving thanks for all your blessings, in a blessing. I think you may be able to obtain holy water from some churches, and even have it sent to you from Lourdes. Holy water plays a big part in the work that I do, and it has always worked for me.

3) What you can also do is connect with those spirits that are within your home. Yes, talk to them, they will hear you fine. Ask them to leave your home in the name of Jesus, (this is my preference, you may wish to call on God, or some other deity according to your own beliefs), repeating that the home belongs to your family now. Ask them to move into the world

of Spirit so that they may be among their own loved ones and family.

4) Say the Lord's Prayer (again my choice of prayer) when you finish connecting with the spirit energy or energies and again ask God to cleanse your home. Saying the Lord's Prayer has more power than you may realise. Many people have attested to its power when they have felt challenged or at times of crisis. It is also a prayer of thanksgiving.

5) Be firm when asking a spirit to leave your home. After all, you are in command and control of your own home, emphasise the fact. It is about being strong in what you do. If you are there to move this soul on let them know through the way you speak and through the words you use that you are not somebody who will back down. You can say to them: "This is going to happen and this is going to happen today, you are going to go."

It is about being forceful but being nice at the same time. Most people in the Spirit world still have the emotions they had while they were on the Earth, so just as on the Earth, if you go into a rant with somebody, it will get their hackles up and you will have an argument. But if you go in and say, look this is the problem we have, it is time for you to go, then you will have a much better chance of success.

If you then feel that what you are doing is not working well enough then ask: "In the name of Archangel Michael and in the love of Jesus Christ it is now imperative that you move on. This is not a request now, this is a demand."

6) Read up on 'smudging ceremonies', which is a cleansing method used for centuries by Native Americans, Australian Aborigines and other first

nation tribes. This is very easy for you to do. You take the dried sage and light it - carefully of course - and then wave the smoke throughout the areas you wish to cleanse. Smudging kits can be brought very cheaply and easily off the internet or at some psychic fairs and wellness shows. Choose reputable sources for safety reasons. You only need a small amount of sage to do this, and ideally you should hold the lighted sage in a flameproof heat resistant receptacle. Also, make sure that the floor upon which you are going to walk is clear of any bits of paper etc, because the last thing you want to do is to trip up as you do this.

7) When moving into a new home, you can bless your new dwelling. In your prayer, ask for peace to reside in the home and dwell amongst all that live there. Many homes become peaceful and homely very shortly after administering prayers and blessings.

8) What sort of preparation should you do before cleansing your home? I always say, if you are going to deal with something that you are not sure about, ask for a little bit of protection, say a little prayer, maybe the Lord's Prayer.

You might want to do a little meditation, just to make yourself comfortable and relaxed. Pray to whichever God you believe in, ask for your guides and helpers to be around you, and for the spiritual, heavenly energy to be strong enough to reach the soul that is in your house. And then ask them to move on.

You can, as I have mentioned before, ask for the help and protection of Archangel Michael. He is a fighter if you like, who will stand by you. He is the one who will stand your ground. Notice that in pictures of him he always has a sword. It is the sword of justice, and if there is anything there in your house that needs to be faced he will face it on your behalf.

Lastly, before you set out to do this, prepare yourself mentally for what you are going to do. You are going to be relaxed but firm, making it plain to the spirit that is causing you trouble that it is time for them to go.

Sometimes people have talked to a spirit and said, 'Look this is our house, you can stay if you stop making a disturbance and moving things around.' This may work, but it is your choice. There are times when a spirit only wants to visit for a while. But you know and I know that the place where a spirit belongs is in the next world, which is why it is preferable to help a spirit move there.

My medium friends and I know that these practices that I have outlined work. Ninety nine times out of a hundred when people do what I have been talking about here, they say to me, "it's got a lot quieter since we did what you suggested." Sometimes we don't get any direct feedback, but then some time later we meet a friend of the person who has called us and they tell us that everything has been sorted out and the house is peaceful.

There are occasions when we as mediums work jointly with the home owner to clear and cleanse a house. For example, someone will ring me up and tell me what the problem is, and I will decide that rather than diving in and saying, "Yes I will come over," I will say something such as, "If you are happy to work with me, then I can do this remotely." I will then work with prayer and imagine the house, linking with the energies that are there and try to establish where there is a problem. I often do this with another medium. If we can't get a good link with the house from talking to the owner then we'll ask them to send a floor plan of the house. Then with that plan we will go through every room with our psychic senses open and our guides with us, and if we get to somewhere where we feel there is a blockage we know there's a problem there, and then we will move around and see if there is a another blockage somewhere else. Then we will fill that area with light and prayer and ask for those that are with us to help clear it. That is what we can do over the phone, and we ask the homeowner to flood the offending area with light and love as we are doing that.

If the disturbance is so serious that the homeowner feels threatened, for example, if objects are being thrown around or the noises become more oppressive then we will visit. In that kind of situation it is not advisable for the homeowner to try and sort things out themselves. It is time for someone like myself or my fellow mediums to come in, simply because we won't run away, whereas those in the house will. We have known a number of people that have left their homes, because of what has been going on for so long. We come in and deal with the problem and the homeowner goes back. Those are the worst cases but they are rare.

So if you feel that you have a problem with some spirit present in your home, try to deal with it yourself as I have suggested, unless of course you feel really threatened. I am sure you will do just fine, especially if you remember that you have guides and helpers working with you, assisting you from day to day. Think of them as guardian angels, it is easier *that way.*

I would like to say once again that we all have the same psychic abilities. We all sense things, feel things and hear things throughout our lives. Whether we choose to develop these abilities or not, they are within us all and we have the opportunity to use them for personal and spiritual growth alike.

Chapter 13

Mapping the World
of Clairvoyance

As much as Spirit rescue, or as some like to call it exorcism, can seem very exciting and important it is only a small part of my work. My role as a medium touches many areas. The world of clairvoyance is a vast and varied landscape, and I believe I have touched every part of the territory.

Through my work as a medium I think I have experienced every emotion you can imagine; the information and encounters that have been relived by spiritual beings through me are proof and truth of a soul's existence after this life. This experience for me has been phenomenal. Through fits of laughter and floods of tears these souls have been able to recreate events and memories for their listeners here on Earth, and in doing so I have had to experience not only their joys but their pain and sadness to provide the proof and truth of the continued existence of life to believers and non-believers alike.

I have experienced the relief of leaving behind a

debilitating pain and illness after exiting this mortal body, and also the sadness and regrets of those who passed suddenly by their own hand or through the fault of another. Yet each and every one of these experiences, no matter how painful and confusing they were at the time or afterwards, have been followed by divine peace and happiness, accompanied by relief and clarity, both for the spirit that is connecting with me and the person or persons they are connecting with.

So many people have been uplifted and re-energised because of those brief moments of time when they were connected with those whom they thought were lost forever from the bosom of their family. Through this proof they have experienced once again the personalities and familiarities of those that have gone before. By proving to you the existence of what we call the Spirit world, these departed souls long to convince you that they are with you at many moments in your life, demonstrating that their love and connection with you cannot be fractured or broken by that we call "death". That which they once were to you, they still are and can be if you will allow it.

When I work with those in the world of Spirit it is not my words that fill the room, nor my laughter that breaks a silence, but those of the spirit connecting with someone in that very room.

Channels Of Connection

As a medium I call on several psychic energies to perform my work:

I am first of all clairvoyant. The word clairvoyant has two parts to it: *clair* meaning clear and *voyance* meaning vision. I see things that are shown to me, which could be an object or the spirit themselves as they link with me. Sometimes I am shown a house or a garden or even a landscape, and sometimes the spirit will show themselves to me set within that larger context. I can't make this happen, it is up to the spirit to show me what they want to show me, but if I am unclear about what I see then I can ask to have some more information. However, very often something that is not clear to me is very clear to the listener.

I am also clairaudient which is made up of *clair*, meaning clear (yes, you're getting this) and *audient*, or 'hearing' and this is sometimes known as psychic hearing or inner hearing". So I receive my messages via psychic hearing.

I am also clairsentient: *clair* and *sentient* which means 'feeling.' I can feel the strong emotions or feelings of people, animals and spirits, and I can also sense the vibrational information of properties such as houses and other buildings, and this comes in very useful when I am engaged in spirit rescue or 'haunted' properties.

There are some other senses which are combined in my work, but I will leave you to explore those, (now you have some homework).

We could take ages just explaining the science behind all this, but for now all you need to understand is that those loved ones that reside in the Spirit world take every opportunity they can to connect with those on the Earth plane whether it is directly through telepathy or through me in a variety of ways. When they are communicating through me they will use anything that they can: pictures, emotions, sounds and verbal descriptions.

Mediums go by many names, some not so nice by those who do not believe, but obviously the choice is theirs if they do not want to believe in what we do. However, I wouldn't mind betting that their loved ones in the world of Spirit get very frustrated trying to get a message through to them by whatever means they can. They just want to say "I am fine,

I live on," but nobody in the family is prepared to listen. Can you imagine how frustrating that must be!

It Is All Very Natural

Whatever method I use for connection or conducting a reading whether personally, by phone, Skype or email, and wherever I am working, be it a church, a hall, a theatre or in my own home, the mode of connection is natural. There is nothing spooky about it. It is the most natural of acts, it is something we do nearly every waking hour of our life: we are communicating, and talking to and with each other and those that link with you from the world of Spirit are talking to you through the medium.

Imagine the Spirit world and the Earth world as two separate telephones, with the medium as the telephone line, get it?. You have a highly efficient and technical line that is capable of conveying pictures, scenes and even emotions to the recipient on the Earth plane. The spirit tells the medium all about the recipient, the ups and downs they are experiencing in their Earth life and then gives guidance and strength to them wherever possible. This is what happens when a departed spirit makes connection with a medium. And as I may have said before it is up to a spirit to decide if they want to communicate with a medium and connect with a loved one or not. A medium cannot command the spirit of a loved one to connect with someone here on Earth, which sometimes disappoints my sitters as well as those who come to see me on stage in a church.

I dare to say that so many clients and friends leave a reading with a new look on life. They often become happier and more confident, with a real passion for wanting to get on with their lives in a more positive and excited manner, knowing that their loved ones in the realms of Spirit are happy, safe and well.

Many clients and friends ask me if I am going to present them with bad news in a reading, or if there is a chance they may get 'told off.' Funnily enough it is the latter concern that seems to worry folks the most. My answer is always a resounding No!! As I have explained, the spirits seek to guide and uplift you, they have lived the Earthly experience and do not seek to judge; through their own experiences they recall how hard life can be and what the temptations can be too.

Your loved ones in Spirit might mention an experience that you are going through, to give you added proof that they are right there with you, supporting you wherever possible. They cannot give you all the answers. After all this is your Earthly journey you are travelling, not theirs, but just like those in your family on Earth they will assist you wherever they can in your times of trial and tribulation, trying to influence you to look at your problems in a different manner. The choice to listen or not to listen is entirely down to you.

And how many of us have wished that we had followed that thought or feeling that seemed to come from nowhere, when trying to make our decision? Where do you think so many of these thoughts and feelings come from? You are being guided. Your loved ones in the world of Spirit draw very close to you, and talk to you when they are making their connection with you.

During a demonstration, whether it is in a hall or church, the spirit that is connecting with the loved one on the Earth may be standing alongside myself or next to the loved one in the audience or congregation. And communication begins by thought transference from the spirit to the medium, which is then passed onto the awaiting recipients. Some spirits link with me through sensory connections; I sense them before I am visualising and describing them. I may sense the height of the spirit when they were on the Earth plane, they may feel taller or shorter than myself, their build may have been slight or rotund, these are all things I can relay to the recipient for verification of the description of the visiting spirit. They may even give me mannerisms, for example, the wringing of their hands, habitual playing with their hair or ear, scratching their hand or fingers etc. The recipient often says to me that what I am displaying in these mannerisms, is exactly what the spirit in their Earth life used to do all the time. When they recognise this I can see the light and smiles in their eyes and the joyful upliftment the connection is bringing to them.

Whenever I give a reading – whether it is on stage or in private – there is a queue of spirits wanting me to give a message to the person I am talking to. What I have noticed is that it is always the go-getters, the most assertive ones, that will be at the front of that queue, while the other spirits – the ones that let others move up before them - get stuck at the back. That is why when I work, I work not only with the spirits who are talking to me, but also with the spirits who are there but which haven't yet come forward. Rather than just leave them there like that I will say to the recipient that I have a gentleman or lady near me, (whom I will briefly describe), but they are not coming forward. Then what usually happens is that the recipient thinks they know who the person is and says yes I want to hear them. I have always found that works. So many times I have had people come up to me after a reading in a hall, and they will say you're the first person who was ever brought in my dad or my son etc. I think that's because I look for people who are around me when I'm giving a reading, and if I see someone hanging back and I know they really want to speak I will do everything I can to encourage them to come forward.

What also often happens is that I am given proof of what the spirit passed with which might be a long term illness or disability they suffered. This kind of information can sometimes be uncomfortable for the medium, because we may literally physically feel some of the symptoms. The pains of a heart attack, the signs of a stroke, cancers, organ failures are all good proof of the information passed from those in Spirit to those they leave behind. All that can be very uncomfortable for a short while for the medium. However, I am one of those that are grateful for those sensations, because generally they are perfect proof of the connection that I am making.

Ahh! I can hear the questions rolling in now. You are of course asking, "Why would someone in Spirit give those descriptions so vividly if they are no longer suffering?." The answer is that the spirit knows that by giving that information the recipient will immediately recognise who the spirit is, especially as illness is so often our last memories of those who have departed. So what better way to remind us of who they are?

Because of the symptoms passed to me I am experiencing and reacting the way they died or suffered, clutching a certain part of my body, maybe having rocking spasms due to the pain, all good visual proof given from the Spirit world. Some spirit visitors give me an almost complete list of their illnesses and passing! Mostly the duration of this discomfort for me is short-lived, but sometimes they dwell on it so long that I wonder after a short while if the symptoms of the heart attack they are sharing, are actually mine, and I have to ask the visitor to withdraw the symptoms, just to make sure. Painful as that kind of experience is, I feel it is all worthwhile for the perfect connection.

Try thinking about what information you might give if it was you connecting from the world of Spirit to someone on Earth. What would you convey? Maybe you had a missing limb, maybe there was a particular phrase that you used to use or gesture you used to make, or your jovial disposition. Really, all you would need to be is yourself with all your mannerisms. After all that's how your loved ones on the Earth plane would recognise you. My personal belief is that your personality is the real spirit you, a huge part of your soul, inclusive of your Earthly experiences, it is who you are.

So looked at in this way, clairvoyance and the messages that mediums are given all make sense. The Spirit world is very much part of our lives whether we realise it or not, and the spirits that communicate with us have lived on this Earth just as we are living now, so they speak to us in ways and with words and feelings that we can understand. That's why I say, it is all really very natural.

Making The Transition From The Physical To The Spiritual

What I have learnt from my years as a medium is that the transition from this world to the world of Spirit is experienced in different ways by different people. Many people that return to their loved ones on the Earth plane during a 'connection' with me, comment that their passing was merely like moving from one room to another room. Some describe the peace that they experienced and the joy of reuniting with their loved ones, and the ending of pain and sadness. Some that passed in trauma have described their momentary confusion caused by the situation that they had been in, while others have mentioned that they needed time to recuperate in a convalescent environment, where they were outdoors in the most beautiful surroundings of sunlight and nature and where the order of the day was rest, as in our Earthly hospitals. This period of rest is short and is meant to enable the spirit to understand that it has moved from one realm to the other.

Some trauma can be caused by fears about the hereafter as a result of religious belief, while other trauma can be caused by the shock of leaving an accumulation of material wealth or even some prized possession on the Earth plane. So don't get too attached to that bank balance or your old rocking chair, although the latter can be reproduced for you in Spirit if it aids the comprehension of your transition, (makes you feel at home if you like) but you will not need it for long, I promise you that.

When you enter the world of Spirit you are back home - home where your journey to your Earthly experience began, and home for its completion. You have time to reflect on your life's journey, time to reunite with your spirit family and friends that you may not have seen for many Earthly decades. Meanwhile the family and friends you left behind on Earth are all within view.

When I am linking with the world of Spirit I hear how loved ones have adapted to their new life, and how they are keeping an eye on their friends and relatives on Earth.

You Can Make These Connections Too

The connections that I make with the Spirit world you can do also. Now I'm not saying that you will see or hear spirits with the same intensity as I do, but you *can* make and have your own connections with the world of Spirit. Most of the time you will do this through what I call thought transference or what is more commonly termed telepathy. You're probably already doing this from time to time without even realising it.

157

There are examples of thought transference in our own world every day. How many times in thought have you said, "Oh I must ring Mum, Dad or a friend" and in a short while, they contact you first? Your spirit has transferred a message from you to them, and they may even say, "Hi, I just had this urge to ring you". Well, your message got delivered, and this happens time and time again. Why not try this for yourself and send a thought request to another; it will also alert you to who is on your 'wavelength'. Twins are well known for communicating in this way; they will usually know immediately if the other one is unwell or is in difficulty or just wants to talk.

The Spirit world *can* make contact with you using a physical voice even though spirits don't have a voice box, but this takes a great deal of energy. A spirit that communicates with a physical voice does so using vibrational pressures to make this happen. They are using the same principle that a plane uses when it is going through the sound barrier. Many people have experienced hearing their name called out aloud when there are no other people present. Some have even recognised the voice as that of a loved one. One or two people I know have experienced this on waking from a dream.

Whether you speak out aloud or in thought to the world of Spirit, the spirits will connect with you. You do not need a medium or psychic to connect to them, although until you learn how to fully connect (hear them), you may need a medium, or some third party.

One thing I do hear a lot during my private readings, is that the sitter who is with me has been asking a question of a dear one in the Spirit realm sometimes several times a day, but has failed to 'wait' for an answer. Only recently, I was connecting a young lady with the world of Spirit, during which the spirit soul said to her (through me),"Thank you for talking to me and sending me those loving thoughts from the family, but tell the channel (meaning me) what frustrates you the most about talking to me?". The young lady looked a bit puzzled, and then the penny dropped. She said, "Oh, I think she means that I asked her some questions earlier, before I left for work and I finished by saying, "Nan, why do I never get an answer from you, it's so frustrating!" The spirit grandmother replied (through me), "How do you think it feels for us darling? We answer you, but you are already on your heels and running off to work or the shops, too busy to listen." The grandmother made a jokey gesture to me as she said this as if she was slapping the sitter around the ear.

Then the grandmother continued, "Please tell her, to take time out, sit quietly, ask her question and patiently await the reply." She added, "And, when you get your reply, do not dismiss my answer by saying that it's your own thoughts that are coming to mind. Trust what you hear darling, even if you feel it is going against the train of thoughts you already have in your mind."

As in all things, practice makes perfect, when communicating with those in spirit. Keep talking with those that have passed over, tell them how you feel and give them love. Of course I wouldn't suggest that you do this out aloud while in a queue, because for most people someone talking out aloud seemingly to themselves isn't welcome in public places. Yet!

But there are a lot of other places where you can do this quietly making the connection, and then you wait for the answer which may come much later. And come it will if you are open.

Chapter 14

You Want Me to Say What?

As a practising medium, it is essential that I give all of the information that is passed to me from the world of Spirit. No matter how small or how weird it may seem or sound I have to relay exactly what I hear to the person for whom it is intended. There are still times when I am given a word or a phrase that doesn't seem right or even nice, but it is not for me to judge, because although something may not make sense to me or sound appropriate it is always understood – and in the right way –

b y the listener. Such was the case when I was demonstrating at a venue some years back, and it still makes me laugh.

Whilst I was moving from one member of the audience to another passing on messages, I was aware of a spirit gentleman who moved up close to my shoulder who asked if he could connect with me. I told him he was welcome to do so. He then placed one hand on my shoulder and pointed out a small-framed elderly lady seated in the centre of the audience. When I was sure I was with her, I explained to the audience that I had this gentleman with me and that he wanted to link with a lady in the audience.

He then said to me, "Please could you say STINKER to her." Speaking out aloud I said, "Pardon me! Are you having fun with me?" The audience was full of giggles and seemed highly amused. "No", came his answer, "Please pass it on to her". I was a little embarrassed to pass this message on to her, but I know from my teachings that all messages are important and not for analysing or censoring. After all we do not know what the message means to its recipient.

I looked towards the audience and could see that my spirit gentleman was standing beside the lady in the middle of the hall. He beckoned me with a nod as if to say, come on then, say it! I pointed to the lady and asked her if I might connect with her, she replied yes with a smile.

I took a deep breath and admitted that the information I had to share was a little unusual. The audience looked intrigued and I noticed that it made one or two people sit up and listen. Meanwhile, the lovely lady just kept on smiling. "Ok" I said. "I have a gentleman from the Spirit world standing to your right, a tall, happy looking man who has asked me to say **"stinker"** to you. Well the whole hall erupted in hysterical laughter, all except the lovely smiling lady I was connecting with. She sat patiently waiting for the laughter to subside, which it did, just as if somebody had turned down a volume switch. When it was quiet the lady spoke up. "Thank you", she smiled. "I have been waiting seven years for that information, that is what my husband used to call me." This time the hall was filled with oohs and ahhhs and one or two tears also. Again the elderly lady just smiled at me and placed her left hand on her right shoulder as if to cover her husband's hand that was perched there.

The lesson here is that if I or any other channel had analysed or refused this small and seemingly insignificant slice of information, that wonderful lady might have waited another seven years for that evidence from her husband. Or sadder still she might never have received that proof again. Messages from her loved one continued, and the spirit gentleman acknowledged me several times with a thumbs up and a big smile. He confirmed that his name was John and told her he loved her now as much as the first time he met her. Job done, contact made.

There are way too many of these Instances to mention. Just because a medium thinks a phrase or word is an insignificant piece of information doesn't mean that it is. Whatever is given to the loved one on the Earth plane is given for a reason, and in my professional opinion it is not the right of the medium to withhold that. When connection is made all information is crucial. All those who are developing mediums would be wise to remember this.

Many of those connecting from the world of Spirit bring laughter and fun to us with their own familiar brand of humour, and that is great proof of their soul's existence. It is great feedback when the sitter or recipient says to me, "Oh that is his humour alright, or " I am so glad to see she still has her funny way, that is her to a T". The personality of a spirit comes to the fore when they are making a communication in my opinion. They are saying, "Hey, it's me".

And some have a more important message to convey, though sometimes it may sound sad to those that are listening. But those that pass into the Spirit realm do not dwell on sadness but on positivity. Their message contains a sense of relief, of cessation of pain and suffering. They are free.

Chapter 15

Jay's Message for Mum

You might think from all the stories that I've shared with you up till now that it is only older people who come back from the Spirit world to give messages to loved ones on Earth. But age is no barrier for those that want to communicate with those on Earth whom they have left behind. This next little story is a perfect illustration.

Working at a church in London one evening, I was coming to the end of a demonstration of clairvoyance. The chairperson in charge of the evening had told me that I needed to bring the evening to an end, so I thanked the audience for their love and energies that had made the connections possible. As I was doing so I was aware of a spirit energy directly in front of me. I could not see the soul, but I certainly felt the presence. I told the spirit that I knew they were there and thanked them for coming tonight, but instead of the energy decreasing as if to leave, I felt the energies increase, and I was covered with a feeling of apprehension which I felt was coming from this visiting spirit.

What happened next took me aback. The spirit was of a very young man, and he said to me, "I would please like to get a message to my mum." Before I could say anything he explained, "I passed into heaven because of the fire. But I am alright Mum, please don't cry, Grandpa is with me." The energy disappeared as quickly as it had come. I asked a question of him but the connection had gone. I knew that I couldn't leave it there, could I?

The chairperson asked me to close the evening with a prayer, but I asked for a few moments more as I had to deliver a message, and she nodded in agreement. I got up again to speak to the audience. I said that after I had sat down I had a young man connect with me asking to get a message to his mother, he mentioned a fire and wanted to tell his mum that he was here, with his grandpa. I told the audience that unfortunately he had not given me a name, whereupon I was interrupted. "I am Jay," he said. 'Oh he is back,' I thought 'and with a little more vigour.' (I have changed the name of this young man out of respect to him and his family).

I asked the congregation if anybody could link with this information, and a hand shot up. "Yes," said the lady, "I knew Jay and I know his mother, but she is not here this evening.' So I thought, that's OK, job done. Or was it?

Within a couple of days I received a phone call at my home. The lady nervously asked if I was the medium that had worked at a venue in London "last night or the night before." After we had exchanged a few more words she acknowledged that I must be that person. At this point I wasn't clear why she was phoning, but I listened as she began to explain why she was contacting me. She explained that her son had passed in a fire and how heartbroken the whole family were. She said that I had given a message which had been accepted on her behalf, and that she "was absolutely flabbergasted" to realise the message related to her.

I explained to her that I do not generally retain the information I am given when I am working as a medium, but I accepted the contents of the message that she said I had given. She asked if she could come to see me to connect with Jay. Granting an appointment was no problem, but I had to explain to her that I could not guarantee which members of her spirit family would be present, and that no medium or psychic can just pluck a soul from the world of Spirit to make a connection with someone on the Earth plane. Once I had explained a few things to her we agreed on a date and time. Two or three days was all she had to wait - a far cry from what happens these days.

The day arrived and I welcomed Jay's mother into my reading room. She acknowledged that she was extremely nervous and did not know what to expect from the session. So as I do with all my first time clientele I took a little time to explain things: I pointed out that she was not going to see any manifestations, nothing would materialise in the room (unless we were very lucky ha ha). I could sense her nervous tension, as I can with many of those that have sat opposite me for a reading.

As the energies began to build there were a few peaceful moments, and I could sense movement around me. One or two family members made themselves known to me. One was recognised by Jay's mother, but the other was not so easily recognisable. Then another energy came forward: a handsome young man with hair cut fairly short made himself known, and I described the energies to her and exactly what I was experiencing. His energy was so great I felt like I wanted to run around the room without stopping to think or breathe, he was so full of life. That was obviously Jay. His mother broke her silence, "He was always like that.

We used to have to tell him to slow down before he broke something, probably his neck," she laughed.

This young soul then appeared to me on the chair next to his mother wearing a cheeky grin. He played with an earring on her left ear and her hand was immediately drawn to the spot. He knew that she could sense him, "Mum knows when I am around her," he added. I conveyed the information to her and she took one of the tissues from a box on the table that I supply for these moments. She wiped a tear saying, " I like to think I do, but I just do not know, how am I supposed to tell"? I explained to her that she could guarantee that every time he came into her mind that he was telling her that he was around her.

Then a gentleman appeared behind the young boy, placing his hands on the boy's shoulder. The boy looked up at the gentleman and acknowledged him with a smile. As I was waiting for the gentleman to speak, he looked straight at me and said, "I am his grandpa". I passed this message on and continued to describe the gentleman as best I could. "Please tell his mum that I said hi, please."

I conveyed this message and he continued to tell her that he did not have any more pain, and he apologised for being so grumpy before he passed. Jay's mum grabbed another tissue as she could not hold back her emotions. "Bless him" she said, "it wasn't his fault he was a terrible patient." Grandpa looked at Jay and they both laughed at her comment. "I didn't have any pain either Mum" Jay said. His mum buried her face in her tissue. Jay continued "Please stop crying, I am fine now honestly." Jay's mum told me that for his age Jay was a gentleman and always thought of her feelings.

Then the story of the fire began to unfold. Jay said to me, "Please can you tell her that I chose to use the top bunk, it was *my* decision." Mum explained what he meant by that.

Jay had somehow been found in the top bunk bed whereas he had started the night in the bottom bunk bed. This had puzzled Mum and the other members of the family at the time, but now she understood and thanked him for clearing up that mystery.

Jay explained to me that there had been a fire in the caravan they were in when they were on holiday. He said that there was a bunk bed and a single bed in their room. His brother had the lower bunk bed and his sister the adjacent bed. He told of the messing about before they fell asleep. In the middle of their sleep Jay said he woke up to see his grandfather's face. (He had passed some time before the holiday) Grandpa said to me, "Wake the family Jay, tell them to get out quickly."

Jay continued, "I knew it was late as everything was still dark, but I could somehow see where I was going and I didn't bump into everything, which was unusual for me. My brother and sister were woken when I shouted at them and shook them, they were coughing and coughing, but I wasn't, and then I saw everyone outside the caravan but I couldn't go. So I watched them hugging."

What had apparently happened was that Jay had been overcome by fumes and passed quickly, and he had warned the others more or less at the same time. So he was able to see his brother and sister coughing while not coughing himself, because by then he was already in the world of Spirit.

He went on, "Grandpa told me I had been a brave boy, and that we had to go and be safe too. It was hard to go with Grandpa for a second, but he promised we would see them all tomorrow." (Grandpa was accompanying Jay into the world of Spirit). Jay continued, "So I went with Grandpa. Grandpa said we *had* to go, Mum, 'people to see, places to go.' "Oh my God", said Jay's mother. "That was Dad's saying." "Love you both," Mum said.

I watched Jay get off his seat and walk around my room. He dislodged a greetings card from my shelf and it fell to the floor. He grinned his cheeky grin one more time, as if to say 'sorry I cannot pick it up!'. His mother jumped as the card fell to the ground. She looked at me questioningly and said: "Jay"? "Yes", I replied, "he is looking around." Mum said out loud: "Don't touch the ornaments for goodness sake" and we all laughed.

Still wandering around the room Jay said, "Tell Mum, she can give those toys away to make some children happy." His mother acknowledged that she had been sorting toys from the cupboard and was putting them into boxes. She promised to fulfill his wish and give some away. "Not all of them though" she added.

It was a good session, and Jay displayed how happy he was with his grandpa, and that they were always side by side. Jay also acknowledged that his grandpa was teaching him many things and showing him many great places in the Spirit world. As the evening came to a close Jay told his mum that he had visited her many times in her dreams. His mother mentioned that she wasn't sure it was a visit, but he had been in her dreams. I explained to her that spirits visit us in our dream state to lessen any fear and anxiety that may be present in our life at the time. Jay kissed his Mum's cheek and blew her kisses of which I informed her. She took another tissue apologising for using so many. Again Jay asked her not to cry, or dwell on how he left. "Remember me as you are doing now Mum," he asked me to pass on to her.

As Jay and his grandpa left the session Jay shouted out, "I am sending you a gift Mum." And on that note they left. Next day Jay's mother met her neighbour, who was carrying a bouquet of flowers that she had been given. They said their greetings and then each of them went on their way, but then after the neighbour had walked on a few steps, she turned back to Jay's mum. She removed the one rose that was in the bouquet and gave it to her. Then she said, "I don't know why, but I have this overwhelming urge to give you this rose, I really don't know why." That was Jay's gift to his mum.

Jay passed from the Earth due to the inhalation of smoke on that fateful night. His spirit and his grandpa undoubtedly saved the remainder of the family by waking them in time. This young guy could not be resuscitated, but passed into the world of Spirit and into the safe arms of his grandfather. It is not always possible for obvious reasons for a medium or channel to retain lots of messages passed to them as they are personal to the recipient. I know that as I write this account of Jay's connection with his mother he has been helping me with bits of information that he wishes me to include.

Jay proved in his manner that there was no distress to him in his passing that night. His love and trust in his grandpa was so strong. He acknowledged that everyone was coughing, yet he was not, because by that time he had left this world. He wanted to prove his passing was painless and controlled. God bless this family.

Chapter 16

Canada: Family Reunion and a Surprise

I have been very fortunate to have worked in Canada on numerous occasions. This is where my father grew up and where many of my relatives live today, so it is a place that I return to from time to time both personally and professionally. This next chapter describes how a family member by the name of Glen reconnected with his relatives (through me) from the world of Spirit. The way in which he connected was somewhat a surprise to say the least.

My brother Bob and I had been staying with our cousins Jackie and Dale in their home in Riverview, Moncton, New Brunswick. We then travelled to our cousins Bonnie and Clark in Fredericton, the capital of New Brunswick, to stay at their lovely bed and breakfast, Kilburn House. That journey was to be no ordinary one, which I can still vividly remember to this day.

We were running late after having taken a detour through the beautiful Fundy National Park, (a breathtaking

80 square miles of rugged country and coastline, sporting 25 waterfalls, and the world's highest tides). My brother Bob was at the wheel of our hire car, and I was reading the map with the intention of finding a short cut using the toll gates within the park. However, I didn't expect to see so many of the gates closed and bolted, and I hadn't taken into account the open and closed seasons of the great park.

We eventually had to turn 360° and go back to where we had started at the park entrance. Needless to say my brother reminded me of my map reading expertise many times afterwards during the trip. We were now several hours behind schedule, and our relatives were all getting a little concerned as to our whereabouts in this great country of Canada. I believe our estimated time of arrival had to be extended by nearly four hours.

Eventually we were picking up the highway signs for Fredericton and driving alongside the great Saint John River towards our destination, and pretty happy to be seeing civilisation again after those hours in the National Park. We now only had to cross a bridge, after leaving the highway a little prematurely - not my fault this time - and we were looking forward to getting back to our family.

We crossed the bridge and went down a ramp, and once again the river was alongside us. So far so good. Then something totally took me by surprise. I felt goose bumps running through me and my heckles were up, which normally would not bother me, because over the years this had become a frequent occurrence in my line of work. If I sense some spirit is wanting to come through when I am doing a reading for someone or when I am visiting a house then I may get the goose bumps, which Is my body becoming alert to what is going to come. It's a sort of early warning system. Some mediums get the shivers in this kind of situation, others hear a ringing in their ears. I get the goose bumps.

However, this time what followed was not normal. I was experiencing dizziness and nausea and for a moment I was a little concerned for my own health. My heart was beating so hard that I thought I might have a heart attack. On those occasions when I go into trance my heart is thumping hard, but this felt even more so. What was also happening was that I couldn't breathe properly. I am a bit asthmatic anyway, though most of the time that doesn't bother me. I loosened the collar from my throat because I felt I was almost choking, but of course that didn't make any difference.

I told my brother that I was beginning to feel unwell, I couldn't explain the way I felt, but I knew this was something that I hadn't experienced before. The feeling continued and I felt my whole body was shutting down on me as my legs and arms were shaking and I began to feel as if I might pass out. I think I knew that something must have happened nearby for me to feel this way, but what it was I didn't know. I think I was in too much of a shock.

My brother told me we were very near our destination and he preferred not to stop in the middle of the road. The nearest I had ever felt like this before was after having an out-of-the-body experience, where all control of my faculties had been taken away from me. I could see the big Canadian Legion building in front of me and knew we were only a few hundred yards from our final destination. How happy I was to know that we were about to see our cousins whom we hadn't seen for two years.

We pulled into Bonnie and Clark's Kilburn House Bed & Breakfast, a lovely red brick building and homestead that had been in family hands for many years - a couple of generations at least. My brother asked me if I he should go in and get some help for me. I said, "Give me a few moments and hopefully the symptoms will subside." As we sat in the car, family from inside the house came out into the yard having seen our vehicle lights blazing away. They were very relieved to see us, as we were so over our estimated time of arrival, but not half as relieved as myself and my brother were to see them, after our little escapades. It had been an eventful trip.

After I had sat down at the kitchen table with a cup of coffee and the obligatory hospitality of cakes and sandwiches that adorned the table (Canadians are the most hospitable people in the world in my book) I went up to our room for a lie down. I joined everyone a little later, where of course the topic of conversation was my health, to which I was happy to announce I was no worse for wear after our little experience. Turning my thoughts back to my recent unnerving experience by the river I asked if anything had ever happened in that area where I had felt ill, and I explained the symptoms once again. I explained that I had felt that somebody was trying to 'get my attention' out there. As I said that I felt that my listeners knew more than they were sharing with me.

My relatives in Canada knew about the work that I do, as a couple of years previously I had gone out there with my partner and she had explained my mediumship abiilities to them. My cousins are very open minded, so they accepted what they heard very quickly. After I had finished talking about my experience by the river, my cousin Bonnie said to me, "You have to meet Barb, you have to tell her exactly what you have told us." She added, "It would mean so much to her I am sure." Arrangements were made for a meeting the very next evening if I remember rightly, and the time came soon enough.

The following evening I was in our room talking to my brother in between his bouts of nodding off, (obviously he found the conversation riveting) when I heard Bonnie call from the bottom of the large staircase that adorned this beautiful house. She was telling me that my 'sitter' had arrived, but at that time I wasn't aware that Barbara was going to be a 'sitter.' I thought we were just going to be Introduced. How wrong could I be? I said that I would be with her in a few moments and invited my brother to join us, but he promptly declined.

I walked down the stairs and then saw a large group of people gathered in the sitting room, several of whom waved at me with a welcoming smile. Well, that's nothing new in Canada either, and in any case it was a guest house so a large gathering was normal too. I continued onward and into the kitchen, where Bonnie was toing and froing with glasses of water and coffee cups. Amid this flurry of activity Bonnie asked me how I was feeling and I replied that I was fine, and then Barbara arrived. Bonnie explained that everyone was in the sitting room and had I not noticed them? "I thought they were guests," I quivered, "I thought it was just Barbara that wanted to chat with me." Bonnie gave me one of her big smiles and replied, "Well when they all heard about the news, everybody wanted to be there, it's OK if we join you too isn't it?" I understood everything later when it was explained to me that they were all related.

I took a deep breath and followed Bonnie back to the sitting room, where everyone was chatting away until I came into view, and then it all went quiet. I think there were about nine or ten people there: Bonnie and Clark, Barbara whose husband was Clark's brother and then there were children too. I had only met Bonnie and Clark before, the others I didn't know. So it was a little daunting, as I had just been expecting a little fireside chat.

Bonnie introduced me and explained our family link which was that my dad, also called Roy (I am so proud of that) was her uncle, and that my dad and her dad were brothers - for those of you who didn't work it out quicker!. She told them of the last time I had visited Canada and how I had demonstrated my "gift" to them. She said we had all been up until 3 a.m. in the morning linking with the world of Spirit. Our family members that had passed over were certainly not shy in coming forward for the family get together that evening, with lots and lots of proof of days gone by and much present day information - information that opened a few eyes and stretched a few memories as well.

When Bonnie had finished, the usual questions raised their heads, such as "how did you know you could do this?," and "how long have you been doing this work?" So we went through my story from start to finish in about twenty minutes. There were a few raised eyebrows and lots of laughter. (Laughter raises the energies that we work with).

Then the conversation moved towards what I had experienced at the riverside. As I started to explain what had happened to me, once more I was beginning to experience the same symptoms, and the effort of somebody from the Spirit world trying to make themselves known to me. I had to ask him to be less impatient as I was feeling the nausea swamping me as before, and again the feelings from several areas of my body were becoming uncomfortable, shutting down simultaneously. There was no pain just these confusing ailments. Then I could sense a male spirit to my right.

At this point I started speaking the words that I was getting from this spirit: "I didn't feel anything," he said to me. "I was out of there like a shot," he gestured his thumb over his shoulder. "It did go cold for a moment," he continued. Suddenly he took me underwater, which was a bit of a shock for me. I felt I was sitting in a car in semi darkness, I was breathing normally but I could not see the spirit gentleman breathing, I was very shaky, but he was very calm. Then he gave me a visual impression like a video, I could see people in the water and there was a lot of confusion.

He then spoke again, "I cannot believe that total strangers are in the water risking their own lives for me," and within seconds I was back in the sitting room. My spirit friends showed me his emotions at the time filling my eyes with his tears; the efforts of these young people trying to save him were once again touching him, this time as a spirit. He mentioned confusion at the roadside, and waiting for family to arrive. He told everyone in the room once again that there was no pain at any time. He then said that he was happy and safe, and so happy that his mother and father were standing alongside him along with other members of the family, in this beautiful place he was now in. He also mentioned that there were still things that he needed to learn and that he was being told there is plenty of time to learn them. (When you pass over to the Spirit world you have to learn the skills of the world of Spirit, - for example how to communicate without a physical body - which you are taught by those around you).

He commented on his loving family that were present that evening. He told me to tell them to be happy. Especially Barb. "Be happy and do everything you want to do in life." He asked me to tell his children how proud he was of them. He continued on to other subjects, for example, the paperwork that he had left on his desk, which unfortunately was in a dark place; the paperwork had to be sorted out! There were a few tears showing themselves in the family, and I asked them if they would like me to stop there. But there was a resounding, "No".

At this point I still didn't know who this spirit was. I'm pretty sure I didn't, and I wouldn't have wanted to know, because once people start to give me information that confuses me as it's interrupting the information that I'm getting from Spirit. So there I was not knowing who this man was, yet it was obvious that everyone else in the room did. They were listening on my every word with their ears glued back.

This gentleman continued talking to the family and he mentioned that he was glad that all the family had got home safe that night. He asked the family not to think about how he passed, only how they remembered him and that he would be continuing to help them as much as he could from where he now was. He showed me some spectacles on the table and asked me to apologise for not wearing them; he knew that they had spent a lot of money on them.

We continued passing on the information and there was laughter when he asked me to mention empty paint pots. The paint pots were part of his work and upon mentioning them there were comments from the family. He responded with a middle finger salute at their comments, and although I tried resisting the mannerism he used, it still happened and once again the room was full of laughter at his antics. (I learned afterwards that this was Glen, always teasing and larking around with his family)

Then he drew close to me again and my feet went as cold as ice. Well actually they were his feet really, he was just using me to give more information, I cannot remember if this was something he suffered from or not.

Then there was a sudden change of emotion as I could feel a sense of pride come over me, when he told me to mention that his mother and father were there with him, and that they were still in charge of things. When they were alive on Earth they were in charge and they were the same now in the Spirit world. This obviously gave him great comfort. He also pointed out that when they showed themselves they liked to look younger and healthier then when they passed from the Earthly life.

When I eventually finished, Barbara broke the silence and said, "That was my husband." So it suddenly all made sense to me, why Barbara had to hear my story and why her children were there too. It also meant a lot to Bonnie and Clark, for Glen had been Clark's brother. That was an unforgettable evening. Glen had passed in the month of June, and we were now in October.

As I continue to write this I can feel Glen with me, eyeing over the information I am setting down here and giving me small snippets that he is adding or changing. He knows that his family will read this book, so he is taking this opportunity to give them more messages in addition to those that he gave when we were all together during my visit to Canada. He tells me now to tell his family that he has so much admiration and pride that all the family are together, and that they are there for each other. He says to tell them that life is too short for bickering. "My children are all their own people," he continues, "with their own minds," and he asks me to tell them that the high standards that he was determined they would achieve, they have far exceeded. He also tells me he is constantly around his children and grandchildren and constantly tries to prove his existence around them. "Whenever you need me I am right beside you," he says to me now. He continues, "Tell them that I share my life with my immediate family and siblings whom I love so much." He is also singing away here. The song he is singing is, "Save the last dance for me". I am not sure who this is for but it will mean something to someone.

He tells me he has the dog with him. He says: "Mention the name William".

As he drifts back to the accident he says that his body spasmed, and his full weight bore down on the accelerator pedal, making the car take off like a rocket, and he reiterates that at no time did he feel an impact or pain. "The small ones are the tough ones", he has just shared with me, as he laughs. (This comment is for his family, meaning I know I wasn't tall but I was tough).

Glen: photo courtesy of the family

Since gaining permission from Glen's family to write about the spiritual connection that he made with the family that evening, I have learned the story of the accident that claimed his life.

Glen passed away whilst en route to pick up his daughter from a bus stop - something he had done on many occasions before. After crossing a bridge and onto a ramp in St Anne's Point Drive, in Fredericton, a physical reaction due to a previous medical condition caused his body to shutdown very quickly, and he lost control of his vehicle.

(My own body had experienced this when I had been in the vicinity of his passing on that night when Bob and I were on our way to our cousins. Glen had obviously connected with me as we drew close to where the accident had been. It is my belief that he connected with me deliberately that night because he knew that I would tell the family what I had experienced, which in turn would enable him to tell them that he was alright.)

Glen has explained to me that after crossing the bridge his body spasmed and his full weight hit the accelerator. His vehicle then mounted the grass verge, collided with a small tree and plummeted into the water. As I write this he once again acknowledges the bravery of the young people that dived into the water to try and save him. However Glen's spirit had already left his body by that time, so all he could do was watch from his new state of being.

I would like to share the review that Barbara Kilburn sent to me regarding her recollection of the night Glen Kilburn connected with his family from the world of spirit:

"I knew nothing about clairvoyants, I have never had my fortune told and I did not believe that people could really talk to the dead. Then I met Roy!!

My husband Glen, had died tragically and very suddenly in June. My family and I met Roy in October.

I was nervous when I arrived, but very soon I was chatting, relaxed and laughing. Roy told us how he discovered and worked to develop his "gift". Very soon I was having a 'visit' from my husband. Glen's personality came through in the things that Roy said.

Roy gave a gesture jerking his thumb to the side and said, "It was that quick. He was out of there just like that!" We felt that we were hearing right from Glen, that he had died so quickly, that he hadn't felt pain. He talked about the water and the women who had dived into that cold murky water to try to save him. He was amazed that they would do that. He also complained about his feet feeling cold. Glen always had cold feet. Glen (through Roy) apologised for not wearing the new glasses we had paid big money for. There is no way that Roy could have known that I handled those glasses that morning, and I had said," Well, those were a waste of money."

It came through loud and clear that Glen was impatient to talk ahead of others. At one point, Roy looked uncomfortable and said," No, I can't say that. No, I can't do that!" The gesture and the remark were both things that Glen said or did often.

It was an evening I will never forget, and I will always be thankful that I had this opportunity. I felt that I was given one last chance to be with Glen.

Also, I felt I was given a glimpse of where Glen is now and that his Mom is there with him. I feel he is OK.

The evening with Roy was a turning point in my grieving. I felt some peace and closure - thanks to Roy and his gift. I am very glad that he was willing to share his gift. I have shared my story with others and know people who want to meet him should he ever visit Canada again."

Barbara Kilburn, Fredericton, New Brunswick, Canada.

I am very grateful to Glen's family for allowing me to tell you this story. It was a lovely connection between Glen and his family and a privilege that Glen decided to connect with me on that damp night.

Glen has been so helpful in aiding me while I was writing this, by giving me little bits of extra information for the family to read, and for you to read as well. He wants everything to be perfectly clear. Those in the world of Spirit like to make sure that what they say is completely understood in every detail. And dear Glen is no exception to that.

Chapter 17

Canada: Many Happy Returns

I have returned to Canada several times to visit family over the years and also to be a medium for those that have now become firm friends. My visits to Canada are always very happy times. The year 2011 was another one of those times. I had already received a number of emails asking me if I would contact some of my friends on my next visit. I was more than happy to oblige. In addition I decided to advertise on some local ad sites announcing my availability over the two week period of my stay. It was a very busy time, and it was also to be a very special time in my life.

A lady contacted me requesting an appointment whilst I was in Fredericton, a very special lady as it turned out. If I remember rightly there was a lot of to-ing and fro-ing to try and organise the appointment as she was trying to arrange a time when she could bring a friend who also wanted an appointment. Trying to balance the timing for herself, her friend and myself was not that easy, but we eventually managed to find the most suitable time.

On the day we had agreed to meet I was preparing

myself for the appointment when I heard the outer doors of the porch close, so I headed out to meet my client. I was greeted with a huge smile and a soft voice," Hello, I am Bev Doucette and I have a booking with Roy Mackay." It is unlike me to be lost for words so this was a first for me. She had such a warmth around her, I realised that I was keeping her at the door, apologised to her, introduced myself to her and welcomed her into the room where I was conducting the readings during my visit. She took her seat opposite me and again I seemed to just stare, don't ask me why but she just had that effect on me.

Along with Bev her friend Sandra came too as agreed. Bev and Sandra decided that Sandra would have the first reading. So while Bev sat in another room I did a reading for Sandra, which went very well. I think she was very moved by what she heard.

Then after a short break I began the session for Bev. We talked for a few moments and I very quickly warmed to her personality. I continued to explain the way I would work and moved on with the session. When I give a reading I do not retain much information from my connections with Spirit. What I do remember about my reading for Bev is that I felt as if I had a room full of people standing around me wishing to make themselves known to us. It was a busy reading jumping from one spirit visitor to another. I recall a husband and in-laws coming to the fore, there was lots of laughter and some tears, good tears I have to say. I also recall a gentleman that made me jump as I experienced the impact of his passing, apparently he was a miner and had passed in an explosion. His personality shone through immediately, a happy soul that simply wanted to say hello. All in all I believe it was a very informative session, full of proof and truth of these souls' further existence. I recall numerous times being asked by friends and loved ones in

Spirit to pass on their love and pride they had for her and the way she had conducted her life so far.

After the appointment was over we had a short time to chat and again I experienced her lovely personality. I know that one of us requested a hug, which was gratefully received, I also remember somebody telling me beforehand that she had the title, "Hug Queen" and I was to learn in the years to come that it was a pretty accurate description. Most people are content with just a hello or goodbye, but not Beverly, hers comes with a hug as standard.

We said our goodbyes and as Beverly left she placed the fee on the table and I escorted her to the door. I do not generally check the fee I receive. I prefer to trust people and on occasions some folk do not have the full fee and leave what they can, which I don't mind as it is less embarrassing for them. But as I sat down to close my link with Beverly and her spirit visitors I was drawn to the fee in front of me. It was then that I noticed that she had left too much money, $20 too much to be precise.

I immediately made my way to the front porch and out of the house hoping that she might still be in the vicinity. In fact they she and Sandra were still sitting in the car round the corner in the Kilburn House car park. I ran up to them with the $20 bill in my hand and said, "You have left $20 too much". "I know" Bev replied, "you do not know how much that reading meant to me and you do not know your own worth". Again I tried to give the money back to her but she refused it point blank. She said to me that she was told to leave the extra and that she was more than happy to do so. I thanked her and went back into the house as they drove off.

Moments such as these always stay with me. Kindness never wears thin when you are the recipient. All that evening what she said left a beautiful warm feeling inside of me.

Back in the UK some weeks later, I felt compelled to

email Bev. I wasn't sure what to say, I just felt somehow it was the right thing to do, aww come on you have had these moments too haven't you?

I was pleased to see that she was not unhappy about my impulse for want of a better word and promptly sent a return email. I soon had a happy pen friend and in a very short time we were mailing and chatting on Skype. Oh my God we had so many laughs, she has a lovely sense of humour, and we constantly talked of my returning again to Canada. This was becoming a habit, but of course she was on my mind too, only with a sense of urgency now (blushes). I would return as soon as I could.

In the year following I was back in Canada, and we shared fishing trips, road trips, picnics on the beach and many more fun times. She was the hostess with the mostess. My new found friend was very encouraging regarding my spirit work. I remember her saying, "I have been to other mediums and I have never met someone as good as you. I think you deserve a bigger audience here in Canada," and she suggested some venues where I could do a demonstration. One of these was a local venue, the Wandlyn Inn, in Amherst, Nova Scotia. The Wandlyn Inn is like a motel, only bigger. It has seminar rooms and a lecture hall, and it is used to hosting conferences. So it would be ideal, she said, but I was still feeling cautious.

Back in the UK Beverly and I continued to chat regularly, by now she had become a very special part of my life. She was still so keen for me to do a big presentation. One day when we were talking on the phone she said to me, "I don't know why you don't do this. You'll regret it if you don't do it." She was so persuasive that I said,

"OK let's do it." We settled for The Wandlyn Inn, which I then phoned, got some more information, and we agreed on a date which was to be Saturday 14th April 2012. Having taken the leap of faith, I said to Bev, "How are we going to do this?"

"Leave it to me," she said, which I did.

Preparing For The Big Event

Bev was a godsend, she took on most of the arrangements. For example, there was printing to be organised for the posters and the tickets. The printers and Bev sent me drafts for approval via email. Meanwhile I phoned the venue and made a number of arrangements. I had the easiest of jobs believe me.

Unfortunately at the time the venue did not have the facilities or manpower to sell or distribute tickets, which meant that my godsend came to the rescue yet again, being the personable being that she is, and she set about the task of finding outlets to sell the tickets. What she told me was that in Canada if you are staging an event and you don't have time for a massive campaign you go round to the local big stores and ask if they would put a poster up for you, and you also ask them if they would hold about 20 tickets and sell them for you, and you give them a couple of complimentary tickets. That's exactly what she did.

Canadians are wonderfully innovative people always willing to help, and soon Beverly had found outlets in several towns such as Amherst, Springhill and Sackville. They were so understanding about our predicament, and of course they gratefully received our complimentary tickets. More on that later.

Next on the list was to find a public address system as the venue's system was not suitable for what we needed. Again, Bev said, "Leave it to me." She had a contact who provided us with the hire of a suitable system which we tried and tested shortly after I returned to Canada in late March.

It was an exciting time getting everything together, rushing here and there. We certainly put a few miles on Beverly's car. And it was fun to be driving on the wrong side of the road once more.

I always have been extremely nervous before any presentation, but to feel it 10 days before the event was something of a record for me. After all these years I am experienced enough to stand in front of many people, but the thought of doing this for the first time in another country, had a totally different feel about it. After all if anything went wrong for any reason I could go back to my home 3,000 miles away. But all those who had helped me had to stay and face the music as it were. Yes I know that this is an exaggeration, but this is how nerves get to me and why it was so important to have the love of Beverly, friends and family around me. However, as always once the presentation began and the links with the Spirit world came through, there was no stopping me.

This Is The Day

The big day duly arrived and during the morning we had lots to do, starting with a full English breakfast. Whenever I am away from home I like to have a full English breakfast with all the trimmings, to set me up for the rest of the day. Bev and I arrived at the Wandlyn Inn during the morning to talk with staff about the arrangements of the seating and to set up the sound system. The staff showed us into the hall we had hired and assured us that if the evening became busier than expected, they would open the two big partition doors in the hall which would basically double the size of the hall. I tried to imagine this happening, that would definitely show us the sign of success, I thought.

Beverly and I had a little fun with the hired sound system

that we had collected from the store earlier in the morning. We had of course been shown how to set it up and link it to the roving microphone. Guess whose job it was to pass it around the audience? Is there anything she didn't do? As we connected up the system and threw the switch, it didn't work. However with a few blue words and a discussion between me and Bev, hey presto we had it working. However I was concerned that once the seats were all in place I might be a little close to the amplifiers, which a high squealing feedback at full volume quickly confirmed. I was sure that all the staff at the venue would come running in, but no they let us get on with it and eventually the face mike and the hand mike were performing as they were supposed to. As soon as that happened there was a whoop and a cheer from me and my wonderful assistant. Well done Bev.

We took a few photos, and then had a chat with the guy who came in to set up the rest of the hall, then left him to it. So we had everything taken care of, or did we?

As we were leaving, Bev being on the ball asked where I would be changing into my suit etc to prepare for the evening ahead. We approached the reception desk to ask a very helpful young lady if she would kindly point us to the changing room I would be using for the presentation and she promptly went to check with the manageress on duty. Shortly afterwards the two ladies emerged from the manager's office looking a little confused. The manageress approached me and politely asked me if this request was arranged at the time of the booking and which manager I had met.

I explained that arrangements has been made over the phone from the UK. I was then politely informed that I should have hired a room in addition to the hall. However, the manager assured me that they would resolve this problem before the evening commenced. And true to her word when we arrived for the *Evening of Connection* the receptionist explained that the manager had given me full permission to use one of the cloakrooms as my dressing/ preparation room at no extra charge. The receptionist then offered to show us the way.

This Is My Dressing Room?

After being guided down one or two corridors, the obliging young lady with a cheerful smile said, "Here we are sir, I hope this room is suitable for your needs," and then added that the entrance to the hall was directly opposite. With my suit and clothes in my hands I shouldered the door open. I couldn't help but laugh out loud at what I saw. It was very…compact! No I mean it was small. It contained one chair, plenty of hangers on a rail, secured so they could not be removed easily, no mirror and very dim lights. But "hey" I said to Bev, "I want to change in here not hold a barn dance". Besides, my nerves were starting to get the better of me as they generally do at these times. I placed my clothes down and we crossed the corridor to check the layout of the hall. Wow! I exclaimed. It was an awesome setup. One of the staff had made an excellent job of the seating: he had opened up the dividing doors anyway and laid out all the seats, it now resembled a small theatre. Tables were placed beautifully around the room with white tablecloths and jugs and glasses of iced water. I had to say I was very impressed, and I'll admit I felt a little emotional at the sight. Tables had also been placed at the entrance doors where admission tickets could be checked and sold.

I had approximately one hour to get everything including myself presentable for the evening ahead. Beverly was my compére and master of ceremonies alongside her job as microphone passer. I think she was busier than me at times.

I made my way back to my little rabbit hole of a dressing room and immersed myself in 20 minutes of meditation, along with a few prayers for a great evening, which also allowed a little time for the nerves to set in again and believe me they did. My mind cast back to a popular TV presenter that I had given a reading to some years back, and I remember that at the time we had got onto the subject about the effect that nerves had played in both our lives. We had the same view in that the day we were not nervous before a presentation, that would be the day to change professions, before ego set in, especially in my work where ego means to me Edging God Out.

To me God is my governor, without his help my work would not be possible.

Support From My Guide

Back in my dressing room I was asking for my spirit guide to draw close and let me feel his presence. My guide's name is 'Grey Wolf', as I mentioned some time back, and he is very much to the point. He says it as it is, no going around the houses to make his point clear. When he draws close I feel his strength and character much like I do with all my spirit connections only stronger and clearer. I caught his reflection in the corner of my eye and as I paced the floor of the little room I asked him to assure me that all would go well and it was not long before his calming voice replied to me.

"Of what do you fear my friend," he whispered, "have you not walked this path many times before? Do not punish yourself," he continued, "you work in the purest of light and energy, energies that befit that of a communicator between worlds, a lamplighter on a journey to illuminate the road for others to see. Do you realise that there are many waiting this night in the realms of the Spirit, there are some that wish to connect for the very first time with those they left behind in your material world at the time of their transition, and you are the conduit. They too wish to give their best, to prove their immortality and to show that which you call death is no barrier. They too have emotions, but they learn to turn their apprehension into excitement, and they work hard to attract their loved ones and their family members to be present at this gathering of souls between the material and spiritual planes. It is nearly time." His voice faded and the energy of the room along with the temperature changed and I knew that he had gone ahead to prepare the hall for the connection.

I needed to walk for a moment or two, and left the cloakroom to walk in the corridor. As I did so I was so happy to see my two cousins Jackie and Dale walking towards me on their way to the hall, their big smiles lifted me a lot. It was a quick hello and goodbye along with a warming "you will be fine" from them both. And once more I was on my own.

The venue fills up

I returned to my room and a few seconds later the door opened, Beverly was standing there smiling, "ready?" she asked me. She could tell I was very nervous but she calmly adjusted my suit collar and topped it off by placing a loving, supportive kiss on my lips, I needed that. As I turned away to close the door, en route to the hall, Bev turned me back to face her and with a tissue she wiped her lipstick off my lips. "That's better," she said with her customary smile. She gave me her best hug and we were on our way.

Beverly went ahead as I waited anxiously outside the hall. I could hear the audience chatting happily amongst themselves, hopefully full of anticipation for what was about to be a great evening of connection. I heard my name being mentioned over the microphone and a few explanations of what to expect and how the audience could play their part. Once again I heard my name mentioned and the audience very kindly applauded my entrance, here we go!

I made my way to the front of the hall to a sea of smiling faces, I took a few seconds to adjust the face microphone and made sure I didn't get feedback from the sound speakers and scare the life out of my paying guests. I introduced myself and explained a little about the work I do cracking one or two jokes along the way, getting them to open themselves up to the evening.

I reiterated some of the explanation that my lovely compére had shared and I could feel the vibration of energy rising as those from the world of Spirit drew closer to their loved ones present in the hall. My eyes were scanning the audience, waiting for a hint from Spirit as to which area of the hall I would connect with. I gave a commentary on everything I was doing and seeing. (This helps the audience to become a vital part of the energy raising, energies that the Spirit world utilise for connecting.)

Connection with Spirit began as I was drawn to several

different people in the audience, we were beginning to share laughter and tears. There were plenty of acknowledgements and a few moments where information wasn't quite understood, I simply asked those people to take the information away with them to digest and allow me to continue with the link I was using. (Generally speaking, when a recipient doesn't understand a message, if they share the information they have been given with other family members later their queries are invariably answered.)

Two Memorable Ladies

I connected with one lady who was accompanied by her sister. Well I think that was the case. As she was receiving messages from a loved one she would answer me with a quite convincing No! But then her sister, as I will call her, would give a nudge to her and say "yes we can take that.". So the moments of connection continued with one lady saying she couldn't understand the information followed by her sister saying out aloud "yes we can". I thoroughly enjoyed that connection trying to hold back my smiling. It resembled watching a tennis match looking left and right as each lovely lady had their say. The audience too were trying to be diplomatic with the humour of it all. God bless those ladies, they raised the energies no end.

Connection well under way

The Odd-fingered Gentleman

A tall spirit gentleman drew close to me as I disconnected with the ladies. He asked me to connect with several people sitting together over on my right. As he drew close I described him and received smiles from the recipients. I asked him to give me some evidence that his loved ones could not dispute. What he gave me is something I will never forget.

This great gentleman at this point gave me a middle finger salute. (I suggest you ask someone close for an explanation of this if you do not understand it). He continued with this finger in the air, and I asked the recipient if he felt the gentleman needed to make a point with his gesture; this amused the group. I also asked them if he had an attitude problem in life. They both nodded No and burst into giggles again, at which point the whole audience joined them. One of the group called out, " Can he give you more please". I looked back at the spirit and he said to me, "What do you

197

see?" I replied out aloud, that I was well aware of what I could see thank you, and the volume of laughter in the hall rose up again. I mentioned to the recipients that I must be missing something. Yet again they burst out laughing. Bemused I looked back at the spirit again, and this time there was something different and it was the finger he was gesturing with. This time I noticed that a third of the finger was missing. I shared this with the audience and it dawned on all of us, and this time I was happy to join them all in the laughter that followed.

One of those whom the spirit gentleman was connecting with apologised out aloud to me saying, "He always joked about his accident, where he had cut off a third of his finger with a band saw. He was playing with you, that was his nature." She continued, "Obviously we knew that a part of his finger was missing, thank you, you were so spot on with the information." That was a relief for us all.

I moved on with the evening and connected with a gentleman wishing to talk to his son and telling me that he had passed with problems to his liver. At first the son was not sure about the information I was providing from his spirit father, but I believe later he accepted it once he had talked to his brother. There were then many others I connected with that evening, but there was nothing unusual or extraordinary about them that I now remember - except for one.

The Impatient Spirit

Further on during that evening something extraordinary happened. It was something that I had never encountered before and I have never encountered since, and to the best of my knowledge no other medium whom I have met has experienced this either. I finished passing on information to a young man, and then I began speaking to a lady in the audience as guided by a spirit that wanted to connect with her. I was in the midst of introducing the spirit to this lady when I was interrupted. That is the only way I can describe it.

I heard what I can only describe as a physical voice, not a thought generated voice which is the norm when working with the world of Spirit, but a live physical voice. The voice said: "I want to speak to my daughter." This was said very firmly. I actually turned around expecting there to be somebody behind me trying to get my attention, but there was no one there. I explained this to the audience in case the voice had come from them. But it hadn't. So I continued.

Scarcely a few moments later I heard the voice again: "I want to talk to my daughter." So I said aloud: "I'm sorry, I'm being interrupted here. I'm not quite sure who this is." I then went on and replied out loud to the voice: "I'm sorry, you just can't interrupt. Please can you step back and..." Before I could finish my sentence, she interrupted me again: "I want to talk to my daughter." I tried to carry on but got stumped again by this insistent voice. I said to the audience: "This person is interrupting me again," which by now was very obvious to the audience. They were all laughing. They could see that I could hardly get a word in edgeways without this spirit wanting to have her say.

A few moments later as I continued passing more messages from Spirit to the audience, once more I was stopped in my tracks. The voice was back, and this time it was louder and with what I would say was a more demanding manner. The voice said out aloud to me: "I want to speak to my daughter" and I realised that I had one very impatient spirit lady pushing in for want of a better word. I again informed the audience of what was unfolding, and I said out aloud to the spirit that she would have to wait her turn, and that hopefully we would get to her at some time during the evening. "I want to talk to my daughter" the spirit lady continued. I explained to her out aloud that I could not allow this to continue, and I could see that the audience was quite intrigued at my own little conversation with this spirit. I continued talking with the spirit lady asking her again to wait her turn, but she wasn't listening. So finally I said to her: "I'm sorry, you have to leave because I'm not having you interrupting."

Once again the lady responded with a loud demanding voice: "Well if she didn't want to talk with me why did she buy a ticket? A few moments of peace followed and I informed everybody that our impatient spirit seemed to have left. We continued the evening without any more intrusions and brought the evening to an end on several high notes culminating in a very appreciative applause as I sat down to open a bottle of water right beside me.

As members of the audience rose from their seats a number of them made their way to the exit, but others came over to talk with me. In fact there was quite a queue really and I enjoyed answering their questions. Some asked about their connection from Spirit that they had had, and others asked the familiar questions such as how I started my work as a medium and how I was aware I had this gift. I answered as best as I could and asked them to remember that we are all learning on this Earth plane, that is the purpose of this material journey, and that we are all mediums to some degree.

As the queue was nearing its end I refreshed myself with another few gulps of water. There were now two ladies standing alongside me patiently waiting to talk to me, looking just a little bit diffident, and they both had smiles on their faces. One of them said to me," Hello, I just felt I needed to apologise to you," saying this in a gentle voice. Totally surprised I asked her why? She explained to me that she was absolutely certain that the impatient spirit lady was her mother, and that the way the spirit had conducted herself was her mother's attitude in life. She said, "The way you were talking to her, and the way you were telling everyone what she was saying, she was so controlling, and that is how she was in life." She said that it was always her way to "butt in on any of my conversations I may have been having with anybody, whether that conversation was private or not!" She continued to explain that she felt embarrassed that her mother was still the same after her death.

She also felt that her mother was still ruining her life and bossing her around every day. I advised this lovely lady to request that her mother cease to interfere in her life, and how to take control of her own destiny without further interference. I said to her, "You have to say to her, this is *my* life, I'm not listening to you any more. You go on with your journey and I will go on with mine." We had a nice little conversation and I could see she was gaining strength by the minute.

Both ladies smiled at me gratefully as we finished the conversation, but I felt compelled to ask one more question of her. I asked why she had purchased the ticket. It might seem a silly question, as she didn't get to chat to her mother, but it was stirring around inside me for a reason, and I felt I needed, or somebody needed closure on this.

Her friend smiled at me and leaned down to say, "She was not going to come for her own reasons, I bought the ticket for her so that she would accompany me to the presentation." And as they thanked me again they walked away and I could hear one say to the other, "See, mother got it wrong again".

What an awesome end to an awesome evening. The

last members of the audience were chatting to Bev as they left and I could see them all smiling and laughing happily. One of them said to Bev as they left, "I didn't believe in this stuff till tonight."

The whole evening probably lasted about two hours, 7.30 p.m. to 9.30 p.m., and I reckon I probably gave messages to about 14 or 15 people. One of them was one of the ladies who had been selling tickets for us in one of the stores that Beverly had visited. This lady was so thrilled to have had a message, she was in tears, and said to Beverly, "When is he coming back?" That was a real wow for me, to hear that in my dad's country, from people I may never see again.

Within a few moments the hall was empty apart from Beverly and myself.

We closed a few doors and sat quietly together, drinking the bottled water that may well have been champagne the way I was feeling. We complimented each other on how all our hard work had transpired. We were more than pleased with ourselves.

We decided to leave everything till the morning, the dismantling of the sound system could wait. We needed some rest though we were still buzzing with conversation into the night, but boy it was good to put our feet up.

The next morning in our own time we returned and dismantled the sound system and stacked it away in Beverly's car, ready to return it to the Amherst Music Centre. My thanks to Steve for all his help and patience.

We took time to go to the reception desk and compliment the staff on the excellent job they had done for this my first presentation in Canada, they were very happy to receive the feedback.

That evening I made a lot of new friends and contacts. Many had private readings in the times to come. I love to receive their emails and provide them with Skype readings over the internet.

Beverly and I had a few days to ourselves apart from readings. We thoroughly enjoyed our private time with more road trips and a little fishing fitted in - both lake and beach fishing, thanks to Beverly's son Kevin. I still have not caught a salmon but that is very much on my bucket list.

Time has moved on since those awesome fun days and Canada always frees my spirit in a way that I cannot describe, maybe it is my family link that I am immensely proud of. All I know is that I would do it all again tomorrow without hesitation.

I have also been offered the opportunity to work in America but as yet this has not materialised.

Was My Dad's Spirit With Me?

Working in my dad's country meant so much to me, because in a way it seemed to strengthen my link with him, and it constantly reminded me of him. You might be wondering whether I ever felt his spirit with me at times? Yes, all the time.

There were many moments that I knew he was there. One instance that especially sticks in my mind was the day I went to visit the area where my dad grew up –Nashwaak. I drove there in my cousin Bonnie's car. She had often said to me, "You can always borrow my car if you need to," so this time I took up her offer. I also decided to visit one of my other cousins on the way to my dad's birthplace. Normally Bonnie and I would go together and she would drive, but on this particular day she couldn't come so I went on my own.

This was a bit of an adventure in more ways than one. I was driving in territory that I really didn't know and driving on the wrong side of the road compared with the UK. There was one point where the road ran alongside the river for quite a long way, and where the road is not very wide. Behind me there was a man in a jeep wanting me to go faster. I was trying to keep to the speed limit and I was also trying to work out where I was. I didn't want to pull over to one side of the road with the river so near and with children playing in the water. So with this man on my tail I kept saying: "Dad, I'm not sure where I am, and I have this idiot on the back of my car." And I heard my Dad saying, "You drive at your own pace, you are responsible for your driving, just keep going straight on, you are going the right way, you won't miss it." But I kept thinking, ' I'm sure I'm going further than we did last time,' and Dad kept saying "you're OK." Eventually the jeep overtook me. So I carried on as Dad said I should, and then suddenly I thought, 'I know this area,' and in a few minutes I was in my cousins' road. Dad was with me that day without a doubt.

And then on the big night, was he there? I don't always know when Mum, Dad or Nan are with me, but I know that they were there on the night I was on stage at the Wandlyn Inn. It was Nan who gave me heart all those years ago when I went on to the rostrum for the very first time - having been a medium herself - and she was with me that evening when I was performing at the Wandlyn Inn. Mum and Dad were there too. Of course they were. I could almost feel Dad's hand on my shoulder.

Chapter 18

More Canadian Connections

I have been to Canada many times over the years. I have appeared in public there on numerous occasions and I have given countless private readings as well, but the messages that I have passed on from the world of Spirit when I was there have largely disappeared from memory. In fact as I explained earlier on once I have given a message I generally forget it pretty quickly. This is true of all mediums. So in casting my mind back to some of the wonderful visits I have made to family and friends in Canada I asked my dear friend Lisa what she remembers about those times when I was working as a medium which was mostly in her home.

"I first met Roy several years ago at a public presentation he was giving at the local Recreation Center, here in New Maryland. I have had the pleasure of hosting Roy three times in my home since then. Each visit is as interesting and informative as the last and I am sure the next visit will be no different.

I was a believer that those who pass on definitely have a life to go to and live on once they leave this Earth. At the same time I was unsure what that would look like or how things would happen – I still am. Also, I was always concerned about loved ones, human and animal, that had passed. Were they happy? Were they safe? What I was less sure of was, could someone actually connect with Spirit? I was not a complete sceptic – I felt that messages were definitely delivered in some way, shape or form from the world of Spirit to the those on Earth. I knew this from personal experience: my grandfather appeared at the end of my bed shortly after he passed to assure me that he was happy and fine and that he knew I loved him.

So I knew that spirit communication between those who have passed over and those who are here on Earth was possible and I also knew that there are many people out there who claim to have a gift to bring messages from the Spirit world when in actual fact they play on people's suffering, insecurities and downfalls. Roy was kind enough to show me that there are some people who are extremely gifted in this respect, who have the pleasure of being visited by spirits, and who are able to convey Spirit messages to those who knew them when they were alive.

I will always remember that public demonstration of mediumship where I met first Roy. The meeting at the Recreation Center was coming close to the end and I hadn't received any messages from Spirit through Roy, so I thought that the evening was not to be *my* evening. Then Roy came to the area where I was seated and asked me about rubber boots. "Small, red rubber boots that a child would wear.' Well, that was definitely me. It was definitely my grandparents telling me they were there. When I was a small child, maybe three or four, I had a pair of red rubber boots my grandfather gave me. I loved them, I wore them everywhere! Summer, winter, rain or shine I wore them even in the wading pool – I loved those boots and it was always a cute little story within my family. There were other funny things about the boots that we don't have to share, just things that no one in the hall or Roy would know. He went on to describe my grandparents and a small woman who has appeared in my home each time Roy has come to see us. I was unclear as to who she is until Roy's last visit when my mother suggested it might be my great-grandmother on my father's side."

Yes, Lisa was just gobsmacked that anybody could know about those welly boots from all those years ago.

"After the session, we chatted for a bit and he immediately began to feel like family. I knew the next time he came to Fredericton I wanted to invite him into my home. So I did. I have now done that three times and the door is always open.

Roy's first visit to my home was definitely eye opening - for everyone in attendance.

Roy had only been in the house a few minutes when something intriguing happened. He sat down and began to chat with a few of us before things got started, and then he just started to drift away and watch the front door. We saw an orb that lingered a bit, then went up the stairs. We were thinking it was probably our beloved dog that we had just lost not long before that.

Then the readings got under way.

First, a very, very close friend of our family had just lost her dad a couple of weeks before. She and her mom were supposed to be in attendance but ended up having to miss the evening as they were handling things on Prince Edward Island where her mom and dad lived.

It was well into the session when Roy looked directly at me and said that the gentleman he had with him wanted to give me a message. It was not for anyone else in the room, just me. He went on to say that this man was in real estate and Roy described his passing and the difficulties he had had with his breathing. My friend's dad that had just passed died from a lung disease and he did indeed sell real estate. The gentleman that was connecting with Roy went on to say that there were legal issues that had to be dealt with, and that his family should not give in, that "he had dotted his I's and crossed his Ts," that everything was in order, and that they should not let the lawyer take advantage of them. He also wanted his wife to know that none of this was her fault and she had given him the absolute best care she could have. No decision that she made was the reason for his passing. He then went on to explain that the item they were looking for and needed was in the top drawer of what seemed to be a roll top desk. He wanted me to promise that I would pass these messages along.

After everyone had left – I called my friend and her mom. They had been in meetings with the lawyer and trying to sort out legal matters, and they said that the lawyer had been trying to say that something hadn't been dealt with before her dad's passing, but they knew it had been. His message gave them the encouragement they needed to find the paperwork and sort it out. Her mom, a nurse, had blamed herself for her husband's passing, that she had encouraged him to take treatments and make decisions that ultimately had led to his passing. She was in knots blaming herself. His message helped her immensely.

Lastly, I mentioned the roll top desk. There wasn't one. After a chat amongst themselves they figured out it could have been his dresser which had a rounded front on the top. Shortly after hanging up from them, they called me, in tears, explaining that they went up and opened the top drawer of the dresser and there, neatly folded was a t-shirt that my friend's daughter, his granddaughter, had made for him when she was small that had their pictures on it. It turned out that she had been struggling with his death much more than anyone knew and she felt a bit sad that her sister and cousin had roles at the funeral, but she hadn't and she was left behind. It also turned out that the dresser had been carefully gone through several times and that the shirt was not there before. This was the message she needed - to feel his love and that he knew she loved him. The t-shirt and dresser are in her bedroom and she is now 18 years old.

During that evening, a friend of mine was visited by the spirit of her father-in-law. She and her husband had been divorced for quite a while and his family had basically stopped talking to her, except her father-in-law who loved his grandsons and really liked and appreciated her. He explained that there was a legal battle, and that there was money involved that was owing to her. A few months later I ran into her and she explained that out of the blue one of her ex sisters-in law reached out to her, feeling rather guilty, and that her father's will was being reviewed and that there was money for her in it. It turned out to be $40,000.00 plus. Made a huge difference to her and her boys' lives.

Roy also explained that some spirits were in and around our home. Our house was a new build at the time but we definitely knew things were off. My daughter, only about eight or nine at the time had said several times that she had seen a little girl. Our cat would seemingly play with someone when no one seemed to be there. My son's medals (that were under his crucifix) in his room would move as if someone was looking at them. The door to the garage would open for no reason, we would hear footsteps, etc.

It turned out that there were two spirits around the house: one was the little girl and another was a man who seemed to be a priest. Roy felt that the priest was here to protect or watch over the little girl and that they were harmless. Roy communicated with them, saying nicely that it was time for them to move on, and it seemed that they did as my daughter didn't see the little girl again and things quietened down.

We also used to hear a loud clanging noise coming from out behind our house. It sounded like metal hitting metal. There was no one around to do that. It turned out to be a man whose t-shirt got caught in some farm equipment and he died. There was no one around with him at the time to try to save him. These were from many, many, many moons ago when this property was farmland and a stagecoach route."

Yes, I remember that evening well. There was a lot of fun and laughter. I think we had about eight or nine people with us, and Lisa's house is so lovely set near the woods of this very rural community just south of Fredericton.

"The second and third visits by Roy were just as informative and interesting.

On Roy's second visit in another year, a very good friend of my mother had her uncle reach out to her with a message. She told me that she came here very open-minded and with a clear mind, with no expectations of anyone coming through for her, so she was shocked when Roy began to describe her uncle to "a T", especially since they had just lost him a few months before. Described as a tall, gray haired man who loved to tell stories, she knew it was him. She said he would be the one in a room full of people who had everyone's attention and rolling over laughing with his stories. He told her that her life was in turmoil, she was between houses and she would need to be decisive soon, for her own health. He told her not to feel bad about her decision because everyone would be fine.

As it turned out, she had been struggling with her marriage, her husband's health, other family issues and she was staying some nights at her sister's home as it was closer to her new job and with late hours it was much more convenient. She had been contemplating staying with her sister long term, but felt very guilty.

Her husband's father came through talking about her husband's health. She knew it was him right away when Roy held up his own hand and held down his ring finger saying the gentleman had lost his finger. He said her husband needed to eat healthily and cut back on chips and junk food and he needed to get up and start moving. He stressed it wasn't my mother's friend's fault, and she needed to take care of herself. As it turned out, her husband was eating very unhealthily, had gained a lot of weight and had gotten very sick with his heart, legs and kidneys. He wouldn't get up and move around as the doctors told him to.

This same person at a different visit from Roy had a connection from her aunt who told her "the only obstacle she has is herself". She told her she needed to stop aiding people in their bad behaviour and to stop giving people money. My mother's friend took this advice. She stopped giving these people money and stopped doing the things that caused her to be labelled an easy touch and once she did, it really opened her eyes and it worked out for not only her but for the others as well.

She also took note of all the messages she had had from her uncle, her aunt and her father-in-law and made the move to her sister's home. It has been a good move for everyone.

A friend of my mother brought her sister with her to the session. I can't really remember much about her readings but the one thing that I do remember is that Roy had told her that there was going to be a significant change in her life and it was going to be her year. The big changes occurred when her sister – my mother's friend - moved in with her.

Roy had also mentioned that her little dog was sitting with her on the couch that evening. He described the dog perfectly including his behaviour. She explained that at times her cat acts like her dog did and sometimes she could swear it was him. Roy suggested that she should call the cat by the dog's name and see what happens. She tried this twice and both times the cat responded.

And finally for this lady, Roy brought up a time when she and her husband were walking to her in-laws, just up the road, when they sensed someone just through the trees on the driveway next to theirs. They assumed it was the neighbour's dog. However, when they reached the end of the drive, where the two met, there was no one, just a single set of footprints in the snow going one way. There had been no one there that day on that driveway.

Another close friend of my mother's was here with the lady that we just heard about. We will call her Marianne. Marianne has said to me since that evening that she wasn't sure what to expect and was 'petrified' by the thought of meeting a medium. She didn't want to have any feelings or thoughts about the evening ahead. She was afraid of her foster mother coming through. She has told me that if she had, she is sure she would have left. She and her daughter had both felt the same way, but didn't realise it until afterwards.

Marianne has told me that as soon as she sat down, she had a heavy feeling in her chest. She started to panic a bit thinking it would be her foster mother but it was not. Her uncle was the first to come through, mentioning that she needed to dust off the exercise bike. I don't believe he knew of the bike – but he obviously wanted her to get some exercise. She did, for a while.

Then Roy asked who the speeder in the room was. Marianne was embarrassed to answer, but then he used some colourful language about drifting over to the shoulder of the road and Marianne's daughter "ratted" her out. Speaking about his own driving experience the man commented, "I was a really good driver you know" and she knew it was her foster dad. He told her he is in the passenger seat with her when she drives and has helped her many times, guiding her back onto the road, slowing her down, getting her to "snap out of it". He had a stern warning for her to slow down and not to "wander" because he will not always be able to save her. He mentioned a transport truck, Marianne slowed down, stayed alert and still looked for her passenger in the car with her. He seemed to be hinting that she had had a lucky escape that time.

Roy asked about a man who passed with bowel issues – Marianne's father-in-law had. He was asking why there was such a small picture of him. I turned out that Marianne had a very small picture of the family so his picture was tiny. He had never been in the home they were in at this time. Marianne went home, found some really nice pictures of him and now there is a large picture of just him alongside other family pictures on the wall. Every time Marianne walks by there, her focus always goes to his picture.

Marianne's daughter (we will call her Rita) was in attendance, and Marianne's father-in-law wanted to tell her that he did have a sense of humour, and Roy asked if at times Rita just feels like bursting out laughing boisterously and she said she did. Roy explained it is her granddad tickling her side. Her grandfather didn't really talk much when he was here with them on Earth – not to be mean, just that they didn't have much in common. When he laughed it was a loud, hearty laugh – much like Rita's.

While Roy was talking to Rita, he mentioned books in front of both her and her mom. He said they were very much alike and that Rita would be using a lot of books in due course. I thought this was amazing, because Roy was unaware they were related. They were not even sitting together.

Then Marianne's biological mother came through. Roy described a not very tall woman, always smiling, and Marianne said yes, she is Venona. Marianne later confirmed Roy's description with her biological sister. Roy told Rita that Venona is always with her and that when she feels someone is touching her hair – it's her. She asked why Rita was doing things to her hair like colouring it different colours, blue, pink, green, etc, - and asked if it was because she felt uncomfortable with her hair or was it to get attention.

She also asked Rita what was taking her so long to get to school, that she is smart and she can do well there – "just do it and you will be doing what you love." Rita had been contemplating returning to college to study Vet Tech – she loves animals – and was working in a local vet office at the time. Roy said he saw Venona standing in front of Rita with her arms wide open saying if anyone is going to hurt her they would have to go through her. This made Marianne feel better as she had been worried because the course she would be taking was in a different province.

Roy also mentioned that someone was going to have a baby girl – no one knew who that would be – but news would come soon, and he said that we should stay quiet and not say anything, because the person who was about to have a baby might not know what sex it was going to be. Roy was spot on. A little while later a friend of Marianne and Rita's had a baby girl.

Roy's third visit to us began in a totally unexpected way. A young woman that worked with Rita wanted to come along at the last minute and was visibly quite excited. We will call her Antoinette. It was a surprise to everyone, when once everyone was seated and Roy had begun to explain how things normally go, she started to basically attack him verbally, being very critical and sceptical and compared him to a well-known US medium asking if "this is all about being famous and making money." We were shocked and I must say I was quite angry at the time. Roy never flinched. He was a complete professional and the session started."

Yes, I remember that. She was saying that mediums ask questions, get information out of you and then make things up. But I wasn't doing that, and I never do that. I was just conveying information that I was receiving. I will let Lisa tell you the rest of the story.

"Well, surprise, surprise, one of the first people that came through was for Antoinette! It was her grandmother. Roy asked about a lost ring, "Who lost a ring from her grandmother?," and Antoinette burst into tears. She explained that her grandmother had been very, very close to her and a very important person in her life. She had not been the same since she lost her. Her grandmother had given her a ring and one day she lost it. She hadn't told anyone and was terribly upset and stewed internally every day since it happened. Her grandmother told her it was OK, that her memories were still with her and that she herself is with her every day and that Antoinette was not alone. She also told her not to be rude, that that is not who she is. Antoinette apologised to Roy and there were several more times during the evening when she was in tears."

I think the fact that Spirit came to Antoinette early on was no coincidence. Spirit came to her because she had been so awkward. Her negativity could have destroyed the whole evening. It also shows that Spirit wanted to support me in a very obvious way. The evening turned out to be fine as Lisa remembers very well: she received a number of personal messages as she will now tell you.

"My grandmother came through for my mom and

explained that she carries a lot of stress that she really doesn't need to carry. She said that it wasn't good for her and that she needed to relax more and not feel that she needed to be on top of everything all the time. At the time my mother had been working extra hours due to an illness in the company she worked for, and also because she feels she constantly needs to be overseeing everything.

My grandmother also mentioned that I was bearing a big load that I needed to let go of because things that were happening were out of my control. She also said that I needed to stand strong regarding my illness and its treatment and that she is proud of me.

She also mentioned the dust web in the downstairs hallway, which I had noticed about a week before as I was coming downstairs, but had forgotten about. It was out of sight from anyone that had arrived that evening, including Roy. I took it down that night.

Then my grandfather came through to reassure me as well and that my husband, Jim, is a good guy, "like gold", he said, which is funny because we always called Jim the "golden boy".

My daughter, Alexis, remembers Roy talking about someone with a collapsed lung, that it was going to be OK, that he would get the help he needed and would survive it. A friend of ours we know through another friend did have a collapsed lung and had a lung disease and he eventually got a transplant just in time. He lived for years after that, battling cancer and other illnesses. It was indeed cancer that he passed from just about a month ago.

Finally, I have just remembered that Roy mentioned a Ouija board at his first visit, and asked who had played with one. It was a friend of mine who eventually very sheepishly raised her hand. She and her friend had used one when she was a teenager. Roy then explained that she had actually let in a dark spirit by using a Ouija board but fortunately it had since left her. My daughter remembers him explaining to her and her friend to never touch Ouija boards, and he said how lucky my friend was that the dark spirit had gone."

Yes, I do recall that now. When you use a Ouija board you are attracting the lower, less developed spirits. They will lead you astray. If you want to be in touch with the Spirit world ask to be connected to your loved ones in Spirit, to spiritual guides, and to the angelic realm. That is where the Light is.

Reading all that Lisa has to say has brought back so many happy memories, including the wonderful feasts of home made food that she always provided us. I always seem to put weight on when I go to Canada!

Chapter 19

My Hardest Test

We all have our trials and tribulations on our journey, after all that is what this life is about isn't it?

Some feel that theirs is a heavier burden than that of another. We will all be tested in more ways than one, living, loving, dying whichever way we see it we shall have to experience these emotions. As a medium there have been many, many times when people have come to ask for the aid of the Spirit world for guidance and help. I have seen many of these lovely yet troubled people in my work leave a lot happier than they arrived, because they knew someone was listening to them and understanding them at this low time in their existence.

Just like us, we ask those loved ones around us to listen to our predicament, to empathise with us, love us, let us know we are not alone. It is wonderful to see these people open up to their family and loved ones in the world of Spirit, trusting in them as they always have. And we all deal with things in our own way. None of us are exempt from these emotions.

In 1995 after surviving a triple bypass operation that

gave our wonderful mother 10 more years on this earth with her family, my mother was diagnosed with cancer. My mother was always the strongest person I ever knew and this did not change after the diagnosis was pronounced. Maybe it had to do with the fact that she had raised four girls and two boys on her own after my father passed in 1958. Maybe it was because she was from a long line of strong women from a strong family, and she was Mum, a loving, caring person with a strong heart and faith. To me, it was as if she was carrying on her life as if nothing had changed.

From the moment we were told - I cannot remember at which stage we were informed - like all close families the prayers went up relentlessly for her to be spared this horrendous illness, and like many I am sure, I could not see much of a change in her for a while and maybe like many I was denying this was happening to her. Cancer had taken other members of our family both prior to Mum's diagnosis and has done so since. If any mention of how she felt was raised by me my darling mother would say, "I have done my three score years and ten upon this world and I am ready for your dad to come and collect me when he is ready." She always told us that Dad would come for her when the time was right. She could be so matter of fact about it.

The one thing my mother was very adamant about was that when the time came she would pass in her own home. This was also the decision of us all. As far as I can remember Mum didn't ask much of anyone, so this was a request that we could not deny her.

I was really glad to see that her strength and her faith were carrying her through, she seemed to be Mum for a long time as the illness took hold. Maybe I couldn't think to imagine her any other way. I cannot say how much she shared with my sisters and brother as it wasn't really ever mentioned.

I cannot even remember her refusing to eat, though I am sure this was a symptom, she just went on enjoying her puddings and sweets. Mum often said she preferred the pudding to the main meal. Who could blame her after all the meals she had cooked for us over the years. Time moved on and she gradually lost strength, oh not her mind, that was strong to the end; she knew how to keep us in place.

We made the most of every moment we spent with her and had already decided to make sure we took turns in being with her day and night, especially when she started experiencing the pain and was gradually spending more and more time in bed or the chair. It doesn't take long for the muscles to waste when you are bedridden with cancer, and it didn't take long for Mum to do so and to lose her mobility. There will be many people reading this who will understand the journey of this despicable disease.

We were advised to have help for Mum and we were very grateful to the Macmillan nurses that assisted us towards the end of my mother's time on Earth. All the nurses were brilliant, they always seemed to be there, yet always in the background to allow us to remain the family we were. My sisters were also amazing with Mum, as it was always the girls she turned to. It's times like this that you really realise how proud you are of your family isn't it? The family were now taking turns over a 24 hour period to be with Mum and help her wherever we could. The painkillers were becoming more frequent, and on occasion the morphine she was prescribed would create problems because she didn't realise that while she may have been in less pain that didn't mean that she could get out of bed and walk. Mum on several occasions was adamant that she could get up and go and do something, only to have to be prevented as her legs would no longer support her. There were several times she scolded me for stopping her. I would occasionally assist the nurses when an injection was imminent as Mum seemed to find strength to try and stop the nurses from administering the drugs. I had worked in care for several years and the nurses would often ask me to hold Mum to stop her hurting herself during an injection. I have to say there were a number of times I did not appreciate doing that job, and it still brings sadness to me on occasions all these years later.

As the course of the illness rolled forward Mum would sleep more and more, though we cherished the moments that she was awake, but they became less and less. On several occasions she mentioned that she was waiting for Dad to come and collect her as she knew he would. I would still take every opportunity to give her healing, to ease her pain, help her sleep and calm her moments of anxiety.

We all at this time did not want Mum to leave, but we knew that there was no relenting as far as the cancer was concerned, plus we wanted her to find peace and be painless. We were praying for her to leave the hard life behind and return home to the Spirit world and we talked about the reception she would receive there.

Every now and then one of the family would ask me if I could see any of the family from Spirit around her, if I was picking up anything. I prayed that I would. Mum was now having more time unconscious than conscious, but we still clung to the smiles and conversations however short that we shared with her.

I have to say there were a number of times when I asked whoever was listening from the Spirit world, if I would be allowed to know when she was close to leaving us, so that I could have something I could share with my brother and sisters. All I could think to say to them was that Mum is a tough lady, she will go when she is ready. That didn't help very much! But that was Mum's way, she would never be rushed.

I remember each one of us at one time or another

saying, "Just go Mum, we are all fine." The questions about who was with Mum from the Spirit world, and who could I see were becoming more frequent. I didn't mind, I wanted to give them something so much, it really hurt deep down inside me. On one occasion after leaving my "shift" as it were I came home and sat with a cup of tea. Everyone was in bed and I was alone with my thoughts and a battle raged inside of my head. They were selfish thoughts I guess. I was asking for answers as to why I had been given the 'gift' of mediumship to help others to be connected with their loved ones in Spirit, and yet I couldn't help my own family that were hurting. I was angry, with everyone and everything, I think I felt that in some way I deserved preferential treatment at this bad time of my life. I knew this was wrong and admitted so out aloud. Then a calmness came over me and I fell asleep only to wake up cold and huddled on the settee.

One time we were all sitting around my Mum's bed chatting while Mum slept and quite innocently I was asked again if I felt anybody was around Mum, if I could see our Nan, or Dad. I said sorry to them and made an excuse to get some fresh air, going into the front garden and grabbing hold of the front gate. Again I asked the question as to when I could help my family's pain. I remember tears filled my eyes and I was trying not to break into a full bawl. I remember shouting out as I asked for help from God and the Spirit world. If anyone had passed by they would have thought that I had lost it.

As I calmed myself down, I said to those in the world of Spirit, what is stopping me telling them that I do see someone, would that be so bad? No I thought, it wouldn't. I went back indoors I remember looking at the sky, full of stars, I'd never seen so many stars. I joined my brothers and sisters sitting around Mum's bed. Someone was making tea, and all sorts of family memories were flooding into the conversation. I remember Mum stirring a little and saying something that nobody could translate. I remember being asked if I was OK as my eyes looked puffed and red, I told them it was from the cold air outside.

We continued to talk and it was getting later and later; instead of shifts with Mum it seemed as if nobody wanted to leave her side. As I drank my tea, I was sure that if anyone was to ask me if I could see Spirit around Mum, that I could say yes, I wasn't proud of the thought but it was on my mind. The amazing thing was that the subject was not mentioned any more that night, and the next day when I was asked again, I could not bring myself to lie, I guess that is the right word. I continued to tell them when I picked something up I would let them know. The next night Mum's breathing was very shallow and broken, but she muttered a few words. If I remember rightly we figured she was talking to somebody in the Spirit world. And having a little moan. I told the family I could not tell what was happening. Things quietened again for a few hours more. Then there was a little more muttering about Dad coming for her. Then again all went quiet. Then the most amazing thing happened: as weak as Mum was she moved her head up the pillow, and puckered up her lips up as if to offer a kiss. I said to her, "Hey Mum, who are you kissing?" Mum as clear as day replied, "Your Dad"!

I recall that it was not long after that, that my darling Mother stopped breathing and transitioned from this mortal and material world into the world of Spirit. Finally my Mum had been given her wish of many years that the man she had loved all her life, had come to collect her to escort her home. It was the most beautiful moment of my life. And I thought for a second how impatient Dad may have been waiting for this moment to come. Mum looked so peaceful, she always had a great complexion but she looked like a porcelain doll absolutely beautiful.

I thanked God for this moment, and I suddenly felt Spirit people around me again. All this time I had felt they were not communicating with me and now they seemed to be back. I heard somebody say to me: "We cannot make decisions for you, we cannot shorten or lengthen the time of transition, they have their free will, they will choose the time."

I also remember the thought coming to me that, had I denied my teachings, my mother's final moments before she passed would have been lost. That moment when she offered up her kiss to the man she loved, was the moment when everybody finally knew that my father had come to collect the love of his life too. I could have deprived my family of this wonderful moment if I had faltered from my spiritual pathway. If I had lied to my family (the last people I should have lied to) in order to alleviate their concerns about the Spirit world drawing close to Mum, I would have failed. Thank God I was strong enough in the hardest test of my mediumship and life.

I could hear "the end justified the means". To see Mum link with Dad at the end of her Earth life was to me, a gift from God and the world of Spirit. It was the hardest lesson of my life to see my family in such pain, but the happiest time in my life that we were all there with Mum and Dad when we witnessed another miracle.

One of the earliest disciplines I was taught in my mediumship development was to only give what you get, I had managed to respect those disciplines, and it just goes to show me that I am still learning.

We love you and miss you always Mum and Dad, but we feel your presence every day for which we thank God on a regular basis. That's the way I do it anyhow. As for my test, I would like to believe I passed that one.

Chapter 20

Animal Magic

Did you know that animals live on in the Spirit world? Maybe you do. But did you also know that they can make their appearance when a medium is giving a public demonstration or a private reading? I've seen this time and time again and it can really be quite funny. Now I know they say never perform with children or animals, but if an animal wants to come in during a public demonstration they're going to come in and there's nothing you can do as the medium to stop them. Not that you would, because they always bring a lot of fun with them. I have to say I love animals turning up, and I've seen some pretty exotic ones too.

I can remember one time very early on when I was in Woking Spiritualist Church giving messages to a lady sitting in the middle of the church, when two greyhounds came in with a tall gentleman behind. I remember this quite clearly because they walked straight past me, while I was talking to this lady. At first it wasn't clear who this gentleman with his greyhounds was. But then later a woman said, "Yes he's my dad, he was always walking with his greyhounds.'

Interruptions like this often happen, because the person can't wait to come on stage and be noticed by someone they know is in the audience. This gentleman was obviously raring to make his presence known to his daughter.

Dogs come in a lot, and so do cats. I can remember another time when I was working from the rostrum talking to a lady a few rows away from me and as I was looking to my right a cat started walking along the rostrum. I see cats a lot when I'm working, so I wasn't in the least surprised, but just as I was about to mention it, the cat disappeared and then another one arrived, a real big ginger cat. I told the lady I keep seeing cats, and she said, "Yes I take in rescue cats and at one time I had 14. I had one very special one that passed away," and just before I was about to say to her 'does it look like a Cheshire cat as in Alice in Wonderland,? she said, "I called it my Cheshire cat." And then I told her about the other cat, and she said, "What does it look like," and I said, "It's got a funny tail, it looks like a question mark," and she said, "Oh yes that was Benny, he always had a problem with his tail."

I've seen horses as well – but not on the rostrum! I had a lady come to see me for a private reading. After I'd been talking with some of her family in Spirit I said to her,

"I've suddenly been taken to a place where there is a five-barred gate. I'm on a farm or something like that, and I'm seeing this horse which seems to have a very big head."

She asked, "Can you describe the horse?"

"I don't know what else to say except that it has a large head. Did it have a big head?"

She said, "No it didn't, but I can see where you're coming from. The horse became very ill, its head was swelling, so we had to put it down. It was heartbreaking, and I've always thought that I had it put down too early and that it should've had a longer life."

At that point another family member in Spirit standing next to the horse came forward and said, "The horse is fine. You let him go at just the right time. He would have just got worse and worse. As soon as he came over to us he was fine, he doesn't have anything wrong with him any more."

The lady was overjoyed, "Oh thank goodness, I never expected to hear this. I was worried for years that I had let him go too early."

"You did the right thing. And the horse is happy."

As you can guess that conversation meant a lot to her. The family had had two horses and that particular one was the one that she used to ride.

I've also seen more exotic animals during my private readings such as camels and elephants, but as with the horse I've just told you about, I've not literally felt their presence in the room as I have with cats and dogs and even smaller animals. Maybe my front door isn't big enough for them! When I've seen an elephant or camel in a reading it's because the departed relative who I'm talking with used to ride them.

One of the funny things about making contact with those in the Spirit world is that if they used bad language on Earth they're still doing so in the world of Spirit. This certainly goes for parrots! I've had several swearing parrots joining the conversation when I am reading for someone. Of course it can be embarrassing for the person I am reading for, but at least it means they recognise the relative!

I think one of my favourite encounters with departed bird life was when a yellow budgerigar came and joined us. I was reading for a young lady. During our time together I said to her, "Did you have a budgie that was all yellow?"

"Oh yes,"

"Well it's just landed on the chair next to you."

"I hope it's forgiven me."

229

"What do you mean?"

"I used to let it out of the cage, so it could fly around the room, and then one day I opened the window, it flew straight out and I never saw it again."

"Well, it's here now."

"I'm so glad it's come back. Hopefully it's forgiven me for leaving the window open."

Animals I think bring more joy than people sometimes.

The animals I see the most are dogs. They walk in and out of the room where I do my readings all the time. I was doing a reading for a lady not so long ago, and I said to her, "I've got two dogs here, one passed before the other."

"Yes, that's right. What do they look like?"

"I can't see them, but I can feel them. One of them is whacking my leg with his tail, and the other one is just leaning on me. It feels as if he's just flopped onto me."

"Oh yes he always used to do that, he didn't sit, it would just lean."

I could actually feel the hairs on his back, that's how real he was to me.

Some of the dogs I get are quite characterful, they come with all their moods and funny ways. And sometimes you can get quite a surprise. I remember one lady came in, and with her came a dog from the Spirit world. This happens so often I've got quite used to it. I thought what a lovely dog, he seems so friendly, so I went down to touch him and I said to the lady,

"He's right here next to me."

When I touched him again he growled. So I said,

"That's never happened to me before."

"Tell me a bit more."

"One minute I could stroke it, but the next time he growled."

"Oh that's him alright, one moment you could stroke

him and he'd be happy, and then the next moment if you did it again he would growl. He was ever so touchy. You could stroke him once and that was enough. He was like that with everyone."

I love it when animals come in, especially when you can feel their character, and I always say 'the animals talk to me.' One thing I've seen so many times when someone's dog comes in is that the dog comes straight into the room and leaps onto a chair and just sits there looking at me, and I will say to the dog, why are you there? And the dog will look at me and say 'because I can.' In other words, he was always allowed to. When I pass this on to the person who is with me, they invariably say, "Oh yes, he went wherever he wanted, and when we had a visitor and they went out of the room for a moment he would get onto the chair. And then our visitor would have to sit somewhere else, because he liked a warm chair."

What more can I say. They like warm chairs and I like their warm hearts as no doubt you do too.

Chapter 21

A Few Questions and Answers

I thought I would share with you some of the questions that I have frequently been asked over the years. As you can imagine I have met quite a number of people in my time as a medium, and many of them have asked me about what I do and about the world of Spirit. So here are some of the questions that I keep getting asked. They may be your questions too.

You might wonder - with all the questions I am asked - whether I always know the answer? No, not always, at least not immediately. What happens if I am not sure of the answer, is that an answer is given to me from my guide or from the Spirit world as a whole. Many a time I have been shown that just because I do not have the answer in my head that does not mean that it will not be provided. I find this awesome when this happens because both my inquirer and myself learn from this result, as I am honest enough to share the fact that I was not wholly sure of the answer myself.

When I am answering a question guided by Spirit the

answer that is given is the one that is the most appropriate for that person. So it might appeal to their mental intelligence, or their emotional intelligence or spiritual intelligence. We all differ in terms of how we experience the world and relate to it. Some of us primarily use our intellect to understand the world, building a library of knowledge in our heads, while some of us lean more towards our senses in relating to what is around us, and then there are some of us who rely more upon our spiritual knowledge and awareness. None of us uses only one channel of understanding, but we tend to focus on one more than others. The world of Spirit knows this, so the messages that they give us are attuned to who we are and how we take in information.

Question: I would love to do what you do, but is it only the chosen few that have your gift of linking with the Spirit world?

Answer: In my experience my answer would have to be a resounding No! Now I am sure this will ruffle a few feathers out there, but we are all the same in this world. Yes we are. And as people from all walks of life, nationalities, and genders do this work I believe that proves my point. However, I do believe that in order to get the best from yourself to do this kind of work that you need a little guidance. You need a helping hand from those that have learnt to hone the necessary skills, in other words, a teacher.

It has been my privilege to teach some of those that wished to learn how to connect with the Spirit world. Some have gone on to use their developed skills to help others, while others have sought to use them in their own way and purpose, which is fine. Like many different schools of learning there are disciplines and levels we need to progress through.

As with many forms of activity it requires a level of discipline to be successful in it. This is true of so many things. Consider for a moment martial arts, it requires a great deal of discipline, mental, physical, emotional and sensory. It is not merely a physical activity, but something much deeper than that. It teaches you to be aware of your surroundings, to know what is going to come next and to prepare for it. Something similar is involved when you are working with Spirit, because you need to develop all your senses and become aware of subtle kinds of information that are around you that you are being given.

My suggestion is to start by learning to meditate which is a great foundation for so many things. It helps you to associate with your higher self, your spirit self. To become an efficient channel or medium be prepared to start on a pathway of continual learning, because believe me these disciplines never end, every lane and turning in life will teach you. If you are patient all things are possible for you, and my belief is that my God (or Great Spirit) as a father will not give a gift to one child that he does not give to another.

Question: My loved one passed into the world of Spirit by his own hand and I am told by so many faiths that he is therefore "in Limbo" not allowed to enter the Spirit world until his full life span has been completed, that he had a contract with life that cannot be broken before its end date. Is this true?

Answer: I cannot speak for other faiths, I can only speak from experience and from the lessons taught to me by my guide and teachers. My experience does not tally with those beliefs, with the greatest respects to those viewpoints.

I have experienced a number of people who passed by their own hands connecting with me when I have been giving readings for their loved ones. The greatest part of their communication is to try to explain the reasons for their actions at that drastic time. They want to let loved ones know that they are safe, but at the same time they need to come to terms with the decision they made and the regrets they have in taking it.

Some describe their last moments and the method of disconnection they used. They feel the sadness that their actions have brought upon their family and friends and long to make amends from the world of Spirit. They want so much to say sorry and that they feel the sadness of those they left behind.

As with all readings they want to prove that they are there with the person who has been daring or brave enough to come for the reading. I say brave because when people have heard so many sad things about those who pass by their own hand they almost believe that this is what they will hear.

So the departed soul will give proof and truth of who they are. They will talk about things that they have been watching happen with their family since their passing, showing that they have not lost their love for those they left behind. In fact the distance they have created with their actions usually enhances the emotion they feel. So if one of your loved ones has passed by their own hand, know that they are safe and well. Let them go and you will feel them around you more than you could ever hope for.

Question.: In your experience do animals ever come through when you are giving a reading, and could you tell me if they resent those of us that have had to let them go because they were old or ill?

Answer: This is a question that I have been asked so many times as so many of us are animal lovers. First of all the answer is a great big YES that animals do show themselves in readings, as you will have read in one of my earlier chapters. They were devoted to those that cared for them when they were on the Earth and they still feel the love you gave them, and their love for you does not expire.

They have no hesitation in showing themselves, and their nature remains the same. On a number of occasions whilst working in public presentations I have seen animals running up and down the aisles in the same hyper manner they displayed in their Earth life. Seeing the pets in this clear manner allows me to describe them clearly to the recipient of the message.

I remember on one such evening whilst connecting with a lady seated close to the stage, a spirit gentleman walked directly across my path followed by two lightly coloured greyhounds. I described the scene to the lady in question and she broke down in happy tears explaining that she had prayed and prayed that when her father passed away that he would be allowed to be with his beloved dogs. Her prayers were obviously answered.

I can fully understand the part of the question that relates to what we might term as euthanasia or what we call 'putting down' or 'helping them on their way.' These wonderful creatures shared our lives, accepted our love and gave their love unconditionally, and they accepted our decisions about their welfare. When our pets have health issues, we obviously want to give them the best medical help that is available to us. Just like us, animals suffer from everything from diseases to emotional problems. In their own way they show that they are not well. In my own case I remember some time ago that I only had to look into my dog's eyes to know they were telling me they needed help. And sometimes like humans, our pets are beyond the skills of medical assistance.

Hopefully most animals have had great lives and their ailments are age related, by the time they need to be 'helped on their way'. Our animal friends trust us to do the right thing where their welfare is concerned. At times like these we may take our pet to a veterinarian in the hope that something can be done for them, but we can usually see for ourselves that these loving companions are tired, or not responding to medical treatment. We may even feel that our pet is trying to communicate with us. When these souls are beyond help and suffering day to day it is us that needs to make a decision with the vet's help. If our devoted pet could talk they would probably say,"I love you, but I need to go." I know I felt my animal friends say that to me, when I let them go and be free spirits again.

If you have loved them, as I am sure you did with all your heart, and you have to make the decision to send them on their way, then do not feel guilt, for your decision was in the best interest of the loving creature that shared so much of your life. And they shall be free in a new spiritual body as we will be one day.

Remember, they cannot make the final decision, they put all their trust in you for that.

I was blessed on the occasion of my dogs' blessed release to spirit, (both were 18 years young) that within seconds of their passing I could see their spirit form sniffing around the veterinary surgery as inquisitive young pups once again. There were no ailments holding them back, no old age symptoms of arthritis or respiratory problems. They were free, and I had granted them that freedom from pain. God bless all our animal friends in the realms of spirit, may they visit us often.

Question: After losing somebody very close to me to the world of Spirit recently, I have been receiving conflicting advice as to how long I should leave it before I visit a medium to see if he will connect with me. Some people have said 'at least a year,' and that really upsets me.

Answer: Nothing is set in stone, there are no rules and regulations. A spirit can make their own decisions as to how long they want to take before trying to make a connection with someone on the Earth plane. Some that have passed over very recently will in their own way make attempts to connect. Many people say to me that they know their loved one is already making them aware that they are still around them. They will know this from sensing them, noticing things happening in their home, such as items being moved around from their original place, lights flickering, electrical items turning on or off.

It is my personal experience that the timing for a reading is up to the recipient. You know when you feel it is right, or you feel you are being prompted mentally by your departed friend or relative to attend an evening of mediumship or seek a private reading.

If you feel happier waiting a year, then do so. If you want to try earlier than that then do that. Nobody can tell you when it is right or wrong for you to do this. As far as the spirit is concerned I have to say that I have had connections within a few days of a passing and sometimes before the funeral or even on the day of the funeral. That happened to me recently when a departed husband wanted to tell his wife to go ahead and make all the arrangements as she wanted and not to be bullied by his relatives into making decisions that she didn't want.

Although going to a medium in the weeks after a passing

can be emotionally painful, it can also give great closure and be a source of healing and peace especially where the passing has been traumatic. In such circumstances the spirit that passes over may be, shall we say, convalescing for a short period, as I have mentioned in an earlier chapter. When you visit a medium under these circumstances please be open to all the connections that may come through, and accept the fact that others in the Spirit world will be eager to connect with you as well as the person who has departed. So don't block them out by only wishing to hear the name or password of the recently departed. (Some people agree with their loved ones before they pass that they will confirm their presence in a reading by using a password, but this is something that can be lost when that person transitions to Spirit). Listen openly to all those that enter the session, they may be giving you information about the loved one you seek, and you could be omitting to hear it in your trepidation.

Here's a piece of advice. I always instruct those that are coming for a reading or 'connection' to think about those whom they wish to be connect with a day or two before their appointment. This is a tip that works wonders. I am so sure that the person who has passed gets the message.

Question: Do my family in the Spirit world know that I still love them even though we often argued?

Answer: Yes they do. They do not lose their emotions. Love is an impenetrable force. They do not feel any the less because they are in the Spirit world, though they may see things in a different light now that they are again in the world of Spirit. I am sure there are times that you feel your loved ones so close to you, that it may bring tears or smiles. This can be a sign of their love for you never waning, never decreasing, that they are sharing their love and time with you, guiding you wherever and whenever you ask them to.

Question: I have lost several loved ones in tragic circumstances, passing over through a sudden impact of one kind or another. I feel anguished at times to think they may have gone through immeasurable pain. Is there any way of knowing? I have never had a connection with a medium before. I believe in a God that is a loving God, who would not let them suffer unnecessarily. Am I right?

Answer: On many occasions when I have been giving a reading the spirit of someone who passed in traumatic circumstances has come through. In every instance they have returned to connect to a loved one to say that they did not feel pain at the time of the trauma. The next story is a perfect example of what I mean. It concerns an airman who was shot down in the Second World War.

The spirit gentleman came through to his granddaughter one evening during her reading with me. During the conversation he said to me, "Ask my granddaughter about the question that she has been asking herself over and over for so long." At first the granddaughter was a little baffled by his question and gave me one of those confused faces, the sort that says I don't know what they are talking about.

He asked her if she remembered how he had served during the War, and she replied, "Ohhh, I know what he is talking about." I was waiting for the answer, when he suddenly revealed himself to me in a flying suit complete with parachute. I remember he winked at me. The granddaughter told me that her grandfather served in the RAF during the War and was a navigator, and she said that's how he died. The spirit gentleman seemed to be mouthing her replies as she spoke with perfect synchronicity and his head was nodding as if he was trying to prompt her.

She said, "The question I have had in my mind was, did he feel pain in his last moments"? This lovely gentleman then told me to pass his story on to her, and he hoped it would clear this from her mind forever. He said that his plane had been hit on a bombing run and his plane was limping home to England when he received the order to bail out, which everyone in the plane did in an orderly fashion. But when it was his turn to jump out, he felt restricted as if his outfit had been hooked up on something, "but with a pull" he said, "I was free." However, when he went to deploy his chute nothing happened. He told me that he had tried and tried to open the chute but it failed each time. He remembered some of his falling to earth and he described it as "not a totally unpleasant sensation".

Then the upward draught from his falling became gentler and quieter, it was happening quickly in his reality but slowly in his mind, and he thought of how people had said death comes in slow motion. Then there was total silence and the falling had stopped. He went on to say, though he still found it hard to believe, that he was then lying on a doctor's consulting table or bed. (He was by now in the world of Spirit). He said there was a tall, slim man standing beside him in what seemed to be a very light blue gown. He said, "The gentleman smiled at me and I felt very calm as he spoke to me and said, 'Welcome' and placed a hand on my shoulder. I remember asking him if I had "bought it," and the spirit gentleman just nodded to me. I felt no panic, just a peacefulness I could not describe other than to say it was heavenly. I immediately asked why I had not felt the impact of hitting the ground. In fact I don't remember the fall very much. There was no pain at all I said, and I asked why was that? It was explained to me that my consciousness was blocked, as if I had passed out. In fact that is exactly what happened. It was the opportunity for my spiritual self to be released. I was told that there was no necessity to feel the pain of the fall, the fall belonged to the Earthly environment and I had left that far behind. The gentleman said to me, "The final part of your Earthly experience will no longer be with you, you do not have reason to recall it. There could be no pain as you were safe in the realm of the Spirit."

The grandfather asked his granddaughter to share the story with those that would accept it, and leave it with those that could not. I was so engrossed in the connection that I did not see the granddaughter wading through the Kleenex box to soak up her tears. I think I took one too.

Then the granddaughter asked me to tell him that she could now forget that recurring thought that she had had for so long, and she was grateful for the knowledge that he had felt no pain. I told her, "I don't need to tell him, he heard you."

Question: My husband lost two legs through illness and although it may sound a little vain, I wondered if in the Spirit world he will still be handicapped.

Answer: I don't think it is vain at all. It's a good question with a short and to the point answer. The limb loss you speak of belongs to the physical body, which is designed for the physical world, the world we leave behind when we pass. The new body for the world of Spirit will be different. Although it will look solid to a degree it will not be flesh and bone. So think of it as a new suit with all the parts attached. So yes, your husband will be one hundred per cent perfect.

Question: I would like to ask your opinion regarding the use of a Ouija board, and in your experience are they safe.

Answer: You will certainly get mixed opinions regarding the use of a Ouija board, and my personal experience is to definitely steer clear unless you are with a trained medium to help with the control of the session. A medium can sense negative spirits trying to invade the séance for want of a better word. When you are using a Ouija you are dealing with a situation that you cannot control, and on many occasions this can definitely attract spirits from lower spheres, spirits that would gladly use the Ouija as a portal to create havoc, creating a doorway back into the world they once knew.

Have I ever used one? No, but I have been present when a Ouija was being used, and to put it mildly I was not impressed. I was 17 and serving in the Merchant Navy, when some of the guys made up a Ouija board for a little entertainment. I tried to keep out of it as I felt nervous at the very thought of connecting with disembodied spirits. The guys played around with it for a while, until the glass they were using as a pointer started circling violently and one or two of them said that their finger got stuck to the glass. This went on for a while and the glass became more violent and unpredictable. I drew closer to see what was happening, and without warning the glass left the table and flew right at my face. Although I was directly in its path, the glass went around my head and smashed on the porthole directly behind me. One person said the glass went straight through me. That was the last time I have been near a board, that's for sure. It is well known that Ouija boards tend to attract mischievous and even malicious spirits. This is because when you use a Ouija you are opening up into the Spirit world in a completely uncontrolled way, and then lower spirits will come in and create a portal into their world which is not what you want. Once a portal is opened it is not easily closed. So avoid Ouija boards.

In my work as a medium I have encountered the consequences of people using a Ouija board. There have been a number of occasions where I have been called into a house because the owner says that the house has become haunted, and when I have asked if they have been using a Ouija board, they reply, yes but that was about three months ago. Then I say, how long has all this been going on, and they say, about three months. That is one kind of consequence: physical things happening in the home.

Another consequence is that the people in the house where a Ouija board has been used start to feel different and behave differently. They may become depressed, moody or even destructive. Children and animals particularly can be affected in this way. I have had a case where a very young girl started to behave completely out of character. Her mother was so distressed that she asked me to help. The child said to me, "The man told me to be naughty." I could see him as she spoke to me. That was sorted out very easily, and the child reverted back to how she had behaved before.

I hope this long-drawn-out explanation helps you to arrive at your own decision. For me and this is only my personal opinion...Steer well clear!

In any case there are so many other better ways to be in touch with the Spirit world, such as through practised, disciplined meditation or by seeing a medium. Let me add finally, that contacting the world of Spirit should always be preceded by asking for protection from the God you believe in. Many people also invoke Archangel Michael, who is revered by several religions.

Chapter 22

Acknowledge Your
Loved Ones

It is wonderful to do this work and bring voices from the Spirit world to those that seek an audience with them. It is amazing to see the happiness and relief of those that leave a reading having received unquestionable proof from their loved ones, friends and relatives that they are continuing to exist. I have been bathed in hugs, tears and laughter throughout the years in gratitude for the connection and what it has meant to the person who has just had a reading.

Likewise those in Spirit are thrilled when they are able to make a connection. So many times they ask me to inform a mother, father, son, daughter or friend that their love will never fail even though they are out of the sight of their Earthly eyes. And they will say to me, 'tell them (my sitter) that I have been to see them.' They may tell me that they came to the person in a vivid dream, and when I tell the sitter they will usually say something like 'yes, that was two weeks ago.' So the dream is a way that your departed friend or relative is saying, 'I'm still around you.'

Those in the world of Spirit want you to acknowledge them when they contact you which they can do in a whole variety of ways. The most classic is when you're really busy doing something, and then suddenly you think of your dad or your mum or a song that they used to love. That is them coming to say, "hello, I'm here." All they want you to do is to say "yes I know you're here." And then they're happy. You don't need to say it out aloud, you can say it in your head and they will hear you.

When those in the world of Spirit visit us in one form or another, we may even want to tell this to others. We can tell them that we have seen Mum or Dad in a dream, and you might get a surprise when they say, "yes, I've had a dream about them too." But remember it is not just a dream, your mum or your dad was actually visiting you to remind that they are with you even though you can't see them. So when you wake up in the morning with the thought of someone you loved, send a thought back to them and say, "Thank you for that. Thank you for being with me."

So acknowledge those from the Spirit world when they come to you. Don't ignore them. We Earthly beings love to be acknowledged, praised and thanked, do we not? Well, those in the Spirit world enjoy that too. I am not saying that if you are at the bus stop and you feel your loved ones in Spirit are around you that you should talk to them out aloud in front of a queue of people. Of course not, but send a little thought out, a simple "I know you are there dad." Trust me, your loved ones who have gone, love acknowledgement from you, that you feel them, that these moments aren't wasted. They try so hard to fulfil those - oh so common – requests: "Just let me know you are there Mum, I miss you so much and I wish you would give me a sign." When they suddenly enter your imagination or you sense their presence, maybe it is the perfume they used, let them know that you have recognised that they are with you. When you do that, someone in the world of Spirit punches the air with excitement. They are always so excited when they connect with you. This may give you a little incentive to give something back.

When you have a family gathering like a wedding, or a big party or even just a Sunday lunch, some spirits of the family will often be there. Have you ever noticed that at these events at some point the conversation turns to someone who isn't there? Someone suddenly talks about a mother or father, a brother or sister or a friend who passed over some time ago, maybe years ago. Well, that's a sign that they really are with you, and they really love it when you start talking about them. They tell their friends in the Spirit world, "they're talking about me on the Earth." So when you lay a table for six people for Sunday lunch, don't be surprised if you feel there are 10 people there. But don't worry, you won't have to feed them! Just acknowledge them.

I laugh when people ask me why those in the Spirit world don't give signs that they are around us. Are you kidding me? They never stop giving signs, and reading after reading has proved this to me. I sometimes think, "How do we miss some things?" Even recently a client was connecting with her deceased brother, and he was explaining how house proud she is and how she never stops dusting and cleaning. He explained how she has a place for everything and everything must be in its place.

Like others she asked me why Spirit people do not give signs that are noticeable to us on the Earth. At this the spirit laughed and placed his head in his hands as if totally frustrated. I relayed this to the client and she looked puzzled. The spirit brother said to me, "Please tell her I know she has pictures on the wall leading up the stairs, correct?" Looking confused she answered,"Yes, but he would know that." I felt I wanted to roll my eyes at her, but refrained from doing so. Her brother then said, "Did you not move after I passed over?

The client thought for a few moments and did some working out in her head, "Yes you are right I did" she answered. "So how did he know" was her next question. He explained that he visits her often as she keeps asking him to do and he knows her house very well, and he knows that she is always correcting the positions of the pictures up the staircase. "I do" she said "that's true". The spirit brother then replied, "Who do you think keeps moving the pictures, Jack Frost maybe!" The client muttered something saying she thought there was probably a draft upsetting them. She then said, "Oh my God, that was his saying all the time, he was always mentioning Jack Frost.

She finished this part of the conversation by saying sternly, "Well you can leave the pictures alone in future, you know it annoys me." You cannot win with some people I thought, as we closed. I wonder how many reading this can relate to this type of sign? Are you going to acknowledge it?

One very vivid memory of my own springs to mind from my childhood. As I mentioned in the opening chapter my father died when I was five years old, and afterwards there were many different signs given to us that he was still with us. I can remember so many times waking at night to what I will call a tingling noise. I wasn't the bravest of kids and on a number of occasions I would dive beneath the sheets when I heard it, wondering what this could be. I didn't tell anybody about this for a long time as I wasn't sure I wanted to know what it was. I always seemed to either wake just as it happened or after it had woken me, still to this day I am not sure.

One day I got the courage up to ask my mother if she had ever heard it, and Mum said, "Of course I have, it happens several times a week." "What is it," I asked her. "It's your dad" came the answer, "it's his way of saying goodnight to me." "What does he do?" I enquired further. Mum told me that Dad always took a glass of water up with him when he retired for the night and for some reason he placed a teaspoon in the glass of water for the night. Mum followed this by saying that she was now doing this too. She then said, "On occasion the spoon seems to tap the glass of water, that's your tingling sound, the spoon hitting the glass, your Dad is saying "goodnight."

Some weeks later upon waking up in total darkness and just before the dawn, I lay awake thinking of this and saying under my breath, *"If that's you Dad ping the glass please."* A few moments passed and nothing happened. I was about to dismiss the theory and turned onto my side to try and get back to sleep. Then I heard it for myself and being cheeky I said to myself that I had just imagined what I thought I had heard. Well, I should not have doubted my Dad as it went again, louder and clearer than ever before. I will never forget that moment as it meant so very much to me and still does. And yes of course I acknowledge these wonderful moments, and I am still rewarded with more signs throughout my life. As you will also, when you accept and acknowledge the presence of such spirits in your continuing life. It's a gift to us all.

The Cobweb Effect

Whilst we are on the subject of signs from the Spirit world, I would like to share another one with you. It is one that I am sure we have all experienced at some time or other. I call it 'the cobweb effect,' and you will understand why in a moment.

In the early years of my mediumship development I began to experience an unusual phenomenon, both whilst preparing to work on stage and when I was connecting with my audience. I would feel the flicker of something on my face, as if a hair had just fallen out of place, and when I went to remove it I found that there was nothing there at all. It was a very strange feeling, especially as it would last for a few moments. I would go back again and try to remove whatever it was, because I felt that there must be something there. Has this ever happened to you? It probably has – and there is a reason for it, as you will learn in a moment.

After numerous times of experiencing this strange sensation I decided to ask my Spirit guide Grey Wolf if he could enlighten me. He did and I was so excited at his answer. Grey Wolf told me that I had been honoured to have experienced this and that I should accept that it was something special. Knowing the way my mind works, he knew that he had to say more than that to satisfy me! So he gave me a full explanation. He told me that when those from the Spirit world draw close to us they occasionally touch us, a sign that they are closely connecting with us in love.

He continued by saying that when they touch us there has to be a protective shield between their Spirit energies and our Earthly energies, and the only way that he could explain the shield that they use is by likening it to the fine gossamer-like spider web strands which have enormous strength. He told me to think of a spider's web woven into the finest, most delicate cloth imaginable and placed between the two energies: the recipient of this love and the Spirit donor. Without this shield the effect on the recipient's Earthly body could be very damaging, so the greatest care is taken in all instances. (The Spirit world operates at a much higher vibrational frequency than we do). On hearing this explanation it seemed to me that what is happening on these occasions is that those in the Spirit world are grounding us, and at the same time honouring and reassuring us with their presence.

I think more and more people are sensing that their loved ones in Spirit *are* with them sometimes. I notice this when I'm giving a reading. I only have to think of the people who sit opposite me, and they will say, "I know my Dad has been with me." They may also sense a difference in their surroundings, for example, they may start keeping the house tidier just as their mother used to. Recently a lady came to see me for a reading, and her dad connected with her. He said that she was doing her paper work very well. At first she didn't understand, so he added, "Doesn't it make sense to get everything in line the way I showed you?." Then she realised what he meant and said to me, "Yes I suppose I'm filing things properly these days, whereas before things would get in a mess and I would panic. I'm doing it all the way dad did it." This is not an uncommon occurrence. So when something like this happens to you recognise it and give a thank you.

Can you make yourself more sensitive to those from the Spirit Realm? In my experience, yes of course you can in time and with a little work and patience. But I want to ask you a quick question before I explain one avenue that will increase your awareness.

My question is, "Are you aware of the world around you"? I mean do you notice everyday things in your life?. If you do then you are on your way to improving yourself and your awareness of the world of Spirit.

Here is just a little exercise that you can try next time you are out for a stroll. It's a lesson in awareness, in being fully conscious of your world and what it means to you:

- Notice the plants and flowers around you
- Listen for birdsong
- Feel the peace within you at every breath you inhale.

These are just a few everyday things that we should all be aware of in our everyday life.

Something else you can do: learn meditation, and find time for yourself to do it without excuses. You don't need to make it complicated and you don't need to sit cross-legged etc. I don't know anyone who meditates like that. (There is more about this in the next chapter).

Love your life, be aware of yourself and you will become aware that the Spirit realm is around you. And so much closer than you could have ever imagined.

Chapter 23

Meditation: A Helping Hand

Meditation is one of those subjects that seems to come up a lot in the conversations I have with people. I have met so many people through my work and my teaching journey who are positive that they cannot meditate or they may have started and given up. I can well understand that. It took me some time to appreciate what meditation can do, and more importantly to work out for myself how I wanted to meditate. Today it is very much part of my life. It grounds me, it allows me for a few short moments to let go of the day and live in the moment. The moment I am meditating is giving me five or 10 minutes to myself, and afterwards I can get on with things without worrying.

It took me a number of occasions before I realised that the approach to meditation that I was taking wasn't working for me. It wasn't helping me to find my own deep peace for contemplation and possible enlightenment. I had read many different books on the subject before I realised I needed to teach myself to meditate, and that I could amalgamate all the tips and instructions from the many 'experts' as we shall call them and create my own recipe.

I learnt that I was not all those other people, I was an individual with different needs and expectations, I could not simply clear my mind as instructed by some of the teaching gurus. My mind was busy and unkempt, it was full of past rubbish as well as everyday trials and tribulations that obstructed me in everyday life. I learnt, as with many problems in life, that we need to find focus. And really it's quite simple after a few attempts, it does eventually become clearer, hence the word focus. I do realise that some people have great problems with focussing, which is why when I teach meditation we use a visualisation technique used in so many other forms of teaching.

I created 'meditation journeys' to guide my clients through the fog and into the light, so to speak, into a spiritual journey, designed to help them find that inner peace and tranquillity and much more. In a minute I will describe the journey for you, so that you too can use it in your daily life. This journey through visualisation can be accompanied by soft background music if you so desire, but please be warned to check that the music you choose does not suddenly gain volume at any point or you may find you are unpleasantly awoken in an alarming way, jolting you out of your calm. So the 1812 Overture is definitely a no no. There are so many CDs and tapes out there to choose from, and some are excellent for helping you drift away into your own meditation.

By the way, did you know that the body can go into a mini meditation on its own? I know that when that happens some people say it's a daydream, but any time I am 'out of it' that's a meditation to me. Remember the times when you have drifted away while somebody was talking to you? That peaceful bliss that put you into a staring mode? Remember the people around you drastically waving their arm in front of your face calling: "Hello! Hello! Are you in there.?" But you are in that beautiful, peaceful and warm inner state of peace. And you do not come to until you are ready. That's a mini meditation.

A Meditation Journey

We're going to start a meditation journey. How long should a meditation take? Well, if you are free from interruptions, as long as the journey takes is my answer. So turn off the phones and the computer and let's take a small meditation journey with a guided visualisation.

Prepare yourself in a comfortable place and position, where the temperature is set as you require it, not too warm and not too cool. Sit in a comfortable manner. I prefer an upright chair, but if you are an expert with the lotus position and your legs will be comfortable, you take up that position. Basically, be comfortable, this is your prime objective. Can you lie down on a bed? By all means, though the heat from the bedclothes underneath you may turn your meditation into a nap. It's your choice.

When you are ready to begin, tell yourself, 'I am ready for my personal journey'. Take three or four breaths, not too deep, four or five seconds in length and exhale in the same manner (of course if you need to take shorter breaths for comfort that is fine) allowing your shoulders and muscles to start relaxing.

With your eyes closed and in your own time I want you to imagine that you are standing on the edge of a forest looking into a woodland. The woodland is quite dense apart from one area which has a pathway leading through the forest with the branches and leaves of the trees creating an arch-shaped passage directly in front of you. You decide to venture in. The dappled sunlight shines through the woven branches above you and the leaves on the floor create a soft pathway for your feet to sweep through. You are happy to journey forward and your ears become aware of the sound of the leaves under your feet, it's a soothing sound not unlike the gentle crashing of waves on a seashore. You feel safe and comfortable in your surroundings and you start to notice the creatures and insects around you, squirrels above you scurrying about their own business, a butterfly flutters in front of you and is beckoning you to follow it, and as you watch it fly you are feeling more and more relaxed.

Follow this trail for a few more moments until you are aware of a ball of light at the end of the arched passage that seems to be wafting a warm and gentle light towards you as you approach it. You realise you are coming to the end of the wooded trail and gradually the world starts to open up before you as you approach the end of the forest. Stopping to bathe in the warm light before you, you become aware of four wide marble steps at your feet that lead down to the most sumptuous white temple you can imagine with large white pillars supporting shining white domes that are part of the roof. The light is bright but gentle on your eyes. The entrance to the temple is secured by two very impressive wooden doors that stand tall in front of you. I want you to walk down your marble steps until you are on the same level as the temple and standing in front of these great doors. Take your time and savour the splendour of their power.

As you approach the entrance, the great wooden doors begin to open effortlessly as if they were as light as a feather. You are drawn into the warmth and light of this great building. It has an ambience of peace and love and its energies make you feel even more relaxed than you already are. All around you are masses of doors encased in beautiful white pillars, these doors seem to trail all the way around the inside of the building. You are walking further into the brightness of the temple. I want you to go to the doors that are so prominent, and I ask you to try and open a door, any door, the choice is yours. If the door you choose is locked then move on to another. If you open a door and you are not feeling happy with entering that room then once again move on to another.

When you have opened a door and you feel that the vibration from that room is welcoming then I ask you to enter. Upon entering there will be a spirit person, male or female, the preference will be yours, they are a guide of the temple and this guide will lead you forward to where you may rest and heal and nourish your inner self. Talk to this guide and ask whatever you wish for the few moments they are with you. You will be led to a garden of peace; that garden will be of your own making. On this occasion I will set the scene for you to follow or change as you so wish. You are led to an area that once again is full of light and colour, there are trellises all around with climbing plants amongst which are the most beautiful flowers, there is water flowing and the sound is welcoming and refreshing. There are stone benches scattered around and you are invited to sit and relax to your soul's content amongst cushions of the finest down.

Take your time and close your eyes, absorbing the total peace and tranquillity that has been granted to you, feeling that your very essence is being regenerated. You are aware of others around you wishing to be with you for a short time; they may be members of your family that have passed over coming to give you their love; talk with them and use this time well. After a short while you will once again be approached by the temple guide and with a warming smile he will guide you back to the door from which you entered. Again, take time to ask any questions of this old soul, they may guide you in your further life.

Suddenly you are back outside the temple and the huge wooden doors are slowly closing behind you. Now you must walk up the great marble steps back towards the path that leads to the forest once again. Nothing is an effort to you anymore, you are light as a feather and your mind is rested. As you take the forest path that leads you away from the temple the warmth is on your back, the light fades a little but is compensated by the sunlight shining through the forest branches and leaves. You are becoming aware again of the forest creatures and of the rustle of the leaves beneath your feet. As you see the end of the forest path ahead you will slowly be coming back to the reality and awareness of your material state. In your own time bring yourself back into your physical reality by opening your eyes. The meditative state that you experienced is still with you. Tell yourself you are calm and happy to return to the Earthly state, you are ready to face life as it comes, knowing you can return to your meditative state when you need to.

Take a few moments before you rise and get on with your chores, and especially do this if you want to travel or have to drive somewhere. Give yourself time to return to your everyday awareness.

Remember this is just one of many scenarios I have used, but you can create your own. If you do, create a scenario that fits with your own comfort zones. So if you are scared of heights your focus might not be on the lines of floating off in a hot air balloon high up in the clouds! Just practise when you feel you have a few moments. You can choose the duration for your quiet time and use it wherever and whenever you like.

Learn to use meditation when you feel stressed, when you need to relax. I have used short meditations while in an MRI scanner, and when I have been in the dentist's chair, and also while sitting in a car park waiting for someone to leave the supermarket. There are many ways that you can meditate and you will eventually be able to cater them to your own needs. Make meditation work your way. "How often should I meditate", is another question I have been asked over the years. This can only be a personal choice.

Please do not think I am one that meditates for half an hour every day three times a day. Far from it, but when I feel the need through lack of energy, or having allowed the trials and tribulations of this life to get the better of me, then I sit quietly for as long as I feel I need to. The only regularity I have regarding meditating is that I will always spend twenty to thirty minutes before a reading or public demonstration, to gather myself and remove negativities before I ask to connect with the world of the Spirit. I need to be a clean sheet as it were.

I hope that this will help you to find your inner peace. You *will* succeed with a little practice. Remember, it is *your* personal meditation, it belongs to you, no one can say that your way is right or wrong, it will be your own creation. If I have made this a little clearer for you then I am glad to have helped.

Chapter 24

My Healing Road

I suppose my healing pathway has been as long as my spiritual development road. Way back in the early days of sitting in my first meditation circle we were told that we are all healers and I firmly believe that to this day. Healing is also a form of mediumship, because when you heal you are linking with spiritual energy. There are many views on healing and there are many different techniques. I am going to give you my own perspective based on my experience as a healer.

We are all healers. Those who think that is not true, think back in your life to the many times you have prayed for the sick and the suffering of those close to you or others around the world. Think of the times you have comforted another human being in their times of sorrow or an animal in fear or pain. How you have wiped a child's tears and placed hope back in their hearts. Were you not healing in one form or another? Healing comes from the heart and from the spirit within you.

I believe in Jesus and the wonderful healing he brought

to this world, and the many stories of how he healed those who were in need. For me those stories are an inspiration. However, there are many different paths to healing, and mine is not the only way.

I believe that when I lay my hands on someone in need that wonderful energies are shared with me and the patient, and we are both aware of the divine spark that we are given in those moments. The most prominent of these energies is heat. I feel heat moving through me as it is guided through my hands; it is the temperature of the energies that we as healers are permitted to pass on. Sometimes these energies vary in temperature depending on the needs and requirements of the patient. It has been said to me on numerous occasions while the healing is in progress, that one of my hands may feel extremely warm and yet the other is cold; one of my hands may be hovering over the forehead of the patient and the other at the base of the spine, both receiving different energies at the same time.

I can only explain this by saying that some ailments require different treatments with different energies. When I am giving healing to a patient, I am aware that I am being guided to areas of need by those that work from the world of Spirit, the Spirit doctors and healers. This is the same for so many healers. We are not doctors nor profess to be - that skill belongs to others - but as I have said, we are all healers in our own way. I have been privileged to have shared with the Spirit doctors some wonderful successes through healing. It is our duty upon this earth to help others in this world, to aid all the creatures of creation.

I have worked with many people through spiritual healing and have many friends that swear that their life was improved by the laying on of hands. I have looked at other forms of healing as well, for example, I became very interested in reflexology and this avenue also bore great results.

I remember at one stage of my healing education that some people that were regularly receiving spiritual healing were now attending reiki healing sessions and this intrigued me. Reiki healing has been around since 1922 and was developed by a Japanese Buddhist, Mikao Usui. Since then reiki has been adapted to various cultures throughout the world. It is based on the principle that the healer is a channel for the energies that activate the natural healing process of the patient's body, restoring it to emotional and physical wellness.

In 2009 I decided to investigate for myself and enrolled in a Reiki1 healers course with a lovely tutor named Samantha in Poole in Dorset. The course was held on weekends which worked very well for me as I was so busy with my own work during the week. Together with my dear friend, Lesley Kearley, I signed up and enjoyed a couple of weekends completing the Level One course. It was a very interesting learning journey, so interesting in fact that I continued with tuition until I completed Reiki Master Practitioner level. I can now offer both reiki and spiritual healing. Do I think there is much of a difference between the two forms of healing? It is really up to the recipient to answer that; whatever they are happy with, will be most beneficial for them.

Healing is something that I love giving, I love to see so many people improve through healing, and I have even changed some of the most ardent sceptics of healing to become ardent advocates. Healing does not always need to be the cure for a physical ailment, but it helps to calm the mind and the body, helping the patient to come to terms with their ailments, helping the body to help itself.

It brings a positivity through Universal energies that stay with the body after the healing session is over. It can help with the body's immune systems and thereby reinvigorate the organs. I like to think of it as a detox session for the organs giving them vital assistance to stay healthy and repair where necessary. Healing works on the mind, body and spirit, channelled from the Universal energies that surround us.

Just as I am guided when I am working as a clairvoyant, I am guided during my healing. I do not challenge the guidance I receive, I do not challenge why I am led to heal in one area even though the pain may be in a different area for the recipient. I have faith in the work I do. I do not need the patient to have faith; whether they have faith or not does not affect the healing energies. Once the patient feels the energies and the temperature changes in the areas of the body that I am connecting with, they know that something is happening. Generally after one or two sessions of healing, their belief grows stronger.

Try healing on yourself. Here's how: if possible place your hand a few centimetres above the area of discomfort and after a few moments you too will feel the energy, the heat, the healing.

Chapter 25

More Questions and Answers

I love questions and answers. In my four and a half decades of working with those in the Spirit world I have heard a whole assortment of questions. Usually I have had an answer straightaway, but if not then my Spirit guides have helped me. Here are some more questions, some of which I think will intrigue you.

Question:
In your time as a medium and with all the connections that you have made, have there been many that have passed over that wished they were back with their families on the earth? Do they wish they were still alive.?

Answer:
I found this an interesting question although the person that asked me felt embarrassed to ask it. We agreed in the end that any question is a good question if it results in useful information. My answer is most definitely and resounding "No".

I have never in my life received a message from someone in the Spirit world saying that they wished they were back on the Earth. Of course this leads to a myriad of other questions.

I have been told many times by someone in Spirit, that they had been taken before they had a chance to experience all the items on their bucket list, but they recognised that the fault was not with the Spirit world or the "Great Creator." More than that, it isn't with sadness that they make this comment, but it is to let their loved ones remaining on the material plane to be aware that life is too short to put everything they want to achieve in life on hold. Their message is life is for living, the past is exactly that, time gone by. The future has not been decided and all things can change. The 'present' is exactly what is says on the tin, it's a present, a gift, so cherish it, use it, enjoy it, make the most of everything associated with it. Do not wait until you are home in the world of Spirit taking stock and saying, "I really should have done that whilst I had the chance, how much time did I waste worrying about what never happened." They encourage you now to take the gift we call the present and experience everything that makes you and your loved ones happy. To make the Earthly experience of time, happy and unwasted.

As for missing their families, they do not! Being a Spirit they can be happy in both worlds and can be with their family as often as they wish and as they are needed. They prove this in so many ways, especially when they make a 'connection', which need not be through a medium. When you suddenly think of them out of the blue that often means that they are with you.

The fact that they do not miss not being on the Earth should not surprise us. The human body is a magnificent peace of engineering is it not? However, over time there is wear and tear on the human body, especially when not looked after or as ageing sets in. Think of it as a pickup truck that over time has accumulated a few scratches and dents due to the wear and tear in its relatively hard life. We could say the human body in time suffers the same sort of problems. So it becomes heavy and cumbersome, and as life progresses everything seems to be a bigger and bigger effort, and the human engine cannot live to its full potential. Yet of course it is the perfect vessel for the material journey we go through on this Earth.

The trade-in for the spiritual body at the end of the material journey has to be the best deal ever. The Spirit body has no cumbersome weight and has a never-ending source of energy. The easiest way to describe its form is 'transparent.' Having no physical body it is not prone to the physical emotions such as negativity and it doesn't suffer pain or mental illness. So the spirit is free and alive, which is part of the joy experienced by those who have passed over.

Question:

What was your first ever memory of seeing a spirit and were you frightened?

Answer:

This is one I remember well. I need to go back to when I was about 12 years of age. I was a member of a Boy Scout group at the time and we used to meet once a week at our scout hut which was at the end of a cul-de-sac situated behind a church and there were two means of exit. One was the normal way out along the lamp lit road, while the other was through the graveyard.

On this particular winter evening the troop finished on time at around 8 p.m. and being winter, it was dark and damp. One of the bright spark friends of mine suggested that we take the graveyard route. Several of us said "no, we're not going," and we were labelled as 'yellow,' 'scaredy cats' and the like. So like fools we all agreed to head through the graveyard past the headstones and the large trees and bushes. There were no lamps to light up the darkness for us, but away we went. Two friends and myself took the lead to prove our bravery, and it was only when we were further into the darkness that we realised that the instigators of the dare had in fact decided not to join us and had taken the other route out!

One of my friends tripped on the path edging and ended up sitting on a grave much to his disgust. I recall he got up much quicker than he did going down. He sure got a fright. We laughed nervously and even that scared us. Our voices echoed in the eerie darkness.

We came to a wrought iron gate which we prayed and prayed would be open. We pushed and pushed a number of times before we realised we needed to pull the gate rather than push it. The church was directly in front of us some 30 yards away with its strong stone tower dating back to the 15th century. We could see the street and shop lights glowing beyond it and felt braver, for a second!.

One of the boys with a raised voice said, "What the hell (this word has been changed from its original quote) is that man doing up there?" We all looked up and replied, "who?", "what?", "where?". As our friend pointed up at the tower we saw the shuttered arch window on the side of the building, and there was this person sitting at the window sill 20 feet above the ground. One of the boys shouted something and the person seemed to lean backwards into the shutters and disappeared.

More expletives followed as another boy said, "You made him fall, quick let's go see if he is OK," and we ran to the front of the church to the large oak entrance. In those days the churches were open all the time and you could walk in anytime unlike now when they shut the doors to keep vandals out.

I was the first to open the door, and as we entered I remembered to place my finger in the holy water and make the sign of the cross over me. I had done this many times as a choirboy in this very church, the others followed my actions religiously,(sorry for the pun). We even bowed at the altar before heading towards the back of the church where the stairs to the tower were concealed by a red curtain, behind the large church organ.

Nobody wanted to go upstairs, and it was getting very cold. Meanwhile, we noticed the church door had been left open by one of us in our haste. I stood at the bottom of the staircase and called up the stairs with my brave comrades holding on to the back of my jacket. "Are you OK?" I called, "Hello" I repeated. One of the boys said, "He must be dead". And then another shouted, "The church door is closing." We turned to see the church door, a **very heavy** oak door, slowly closing. We changed direction and ran for the church door but within a yard of reaching it, it seemed to move faster and closed. Dear Jesus, we are still very sorry for the swear words we used in your church, whilst fearing for our lives.

We all got in each other's way pulling at the door, but it just wouldn't move. I had opened that door hundreds of times as a choirboy so I knew how it opened, but this time nothing happened. Then all of a sudden it seemed to open with ease. We ran and ran out of the churchyard all heading in different directions as we lived in different parts of the town. I must have run all the way home, as I seemed to be there in a flash banging on the front door praying for it to be opened. My mother told me off for banging so loud "the neighbours must have heard you." After a few moments my mother said to me, "What's the matter with you, seen a ghost? I said nothing. Next day by the light of the morning sun I went back to the church to have a look around. Did I go up the stairs to check? You have to be joking.

No person was ever found dead or injured in that tower, and I know the organist used the stairs daily to climb up to the organ and practise her skills. That was my encounter with a spirit as I remember it. But who closed the heavy church door behind us, and why couldn't we all strong boys pulling together, open it? Was somebody holding it back for those long but short moments? If there was someone, it was not a human being because once the door was open we saw no one behind it.

Who would have believed then that one day I would be seeing many spirits in my life and I don't mean the type a bartender serves.

Chapter 26

You Are More in Control Than You Think

We all experience difficulties in our life from time to time, and some of these may be long-lasting and ever present. But we always have a choice as to how we respond. There is always a reservoir of positive energy that we can access. The more positive you are the more positivity you will attract into your life and likewise the opposite is also true – if you are negative in your thoughts or actions that will attract negativity of some kind.

I have had friends in life that seem to experience far more trials and tribulations than others, and yet they carry on through life, cheerful, singing, seemingly without a care in the world and when you approach the subject of their troubled life and their attitude to it, they reply, "What is the point of worrying about it? If there is nothing I can do, then there is nothing I can do." "Something will turn up" and I have noticed over time, their positive attitude brings about the change in their life that they needed. "Something did turn up", positivity attracted positivity. Remember this in your life, it will help you without a doubt. "Like attracts like". These are the laws of attraction.

Worrying Doesn't Help You

Does worrying have any purpose at all? The answer to that is NO! Negativity is still an energy and as you can probably associate whenever we worry, that state of mind increases and we worry more. Thus negativity gathers momentum, it not only increases time and time again, but it forms a barrier, a brick wall against what we should be creating... Positivity!

Once again, like attracts like. So by making a choice – minus or a plus, you can determine the way your life will go. Full steam ahead or on pause. How many of us let worry and negative thinking become so heavy upon us that we cannot see our way out of what holds us back? Yet in time, things change, other factors enter our lives. We see a faint light at the end of our dark tunnel of negative vibrations. That faint light is positivity shining through and once we embrace that flicker of hope of positivity it brings upliftment into our lives. Hopefully we can maintain those positive feelings. So just as negativity blocks out the light in our lives positivity blocks out the negative, all things can pass, all phases are temporary. You will look back at the past one day and say, "why on God's earth did I worry? I weathered the storm eventually". And how long did that storm last? As long as you let it reign over that part of your life, that's how long!!

Don't Let Others Upset You

We are more in control of our lives than we give ourselves credit for. May I continue on this subject for just one more moment, and refer to something that affects so many of us. How many times have we done our best for another, maybe a friend or family member? We have helped them through a particularly hard time, we may have given them emotional support, maybe financial or physical help, only to find it has not been appreciated and thrown back in our faces, or they may deny that we had given the time, effort and love that we have?

How do we feel? We feel hurt and angry, sad, embarrassed, unappreciated? You may like me have retaliated verbally with statements such as, that is the last time I help you, and the last time I help anyone. Sound familiar?

Of course a small percentage of us may be able to simply brush this sort of thing off, but the majority of super sensitive human beings will take it to heart. It will of course upset us, it may stay with us for hours, days or even longer. It may even cause such friction that we may sever our links with what we see as the perpetrator.

Once more, control comes into the equation. We are happy to "blame" others, for upsetting us, putting us down. We blame others for the way we feel, long term and short term for our tears and loss of sleep, for our anger and confusion. Conclusion: "it's all their fault". This whole scenario is taking away the control we were just learning about. You have a choice in this wholly sad affair. If you are willing to allow another's actions and deeds to govern your feelings, then you are allowing that choice.

I can almost hear you say "yeah right", I want to be upset, to feel hurt and I totally understand what you would feel, but you have a choice: do you let the whole incident burn a hole in your heart or do you let it all go and get on with your life? Your inner self does not want to bathe in self-pity, neither does it want to retaliate, it wants to find the passive solution, it wants peace for you. After all it's you that feels the victim, for want of a better word. But listen to your spirit. Your spirit tells you that you are above that negativity, you are aware of your efforts and that you need to prove that to nobody! Your inner spirit is so strong, so versatile it can deal with anything. It wants you to progress.

Take Charge Of Yourself

This is your life, your journey, do not allow these tests in life to obstruct that pathway. "You" are the most important person in your life, you have chosen to be educated in the material world, all the experiences you encounter are necessary to you for spiritual progression, both in this world and the next.

Now I totally understand when you say that the most important person in your life is your partner, grandchild, son or daughter or maybe your parents, but again, it is not their journey, they are a part of your life yes, as you are theirs. I know that so many people in your life "depend on you", I can hear you thinking this too. But if this is the case, doesn't it make oh so much sense to look after 'you' even more?

Imagine for a moment please, a large marquee or tent, with one large upright pole keeping the tent upright, keeping the canvas cover off the ground; the ropes and guys taut. Now what if that pole had been mistreated, damaged by weather etc., how long a life will that support have with its strength seriously diminished? You are that pole in your lifetime, the canvas cover is your family and friends, the ropes are your grandchildren. If you allow yourself, as that support to weaken because you haven't looked after yourself well I think you can see where I am going with this.

If you allow yourself to collapse from self-neglect, then all those you support with strength, love and tenderness to some extent collapse in some way with you. Only by being strong for yourself can you be strong for others, and the bigger picture means you are feeling that tender loving care that you deserve. By giving yourself and your inner spirit a new strength, you will be in a far better place both spiritually and physically, and you will be better equipped to deal with the day to day trials and tribulations you may face in your life. Your spiritual journey will become clearer too.

Being More Aware Spiritually Will Help You

Some of the strongest, most grounded people I know are also the most spiritual. This is no coincidence. When you become more aware of the world of Spirit you become attuned to the Creator, the angels, your guides and family helpers in Spirit. From these sources you can receive information, insight and guidance – if you listen. That gives you more control of your life. When your higher self is in communication with these spiritual energies, you have a rudder to steer your life by rather than being tossed about by every happenstance around you. You will still have difficulties and testing times, but if you maintain a link with the spiritual world and its loving energies you will tend to make wiser decisions and feel more in control and at peace.

Chapter 27

Reflections

When I think back over more than four decades of my work, it really is quite humbling. I look how far I have come, I look at the different things that I have learnt and probably would have thought that I could never learn. It's been an amazing journey.

And then I look at the lives that I have touched. I would never have believed that one day somebody would actually turn round to me and say, "'you have saved my life", which has been said to me on a number of occasions. That is a big thing to be able to do. Even in the reviews I have had people have said pretty much the same thing. They say, "you have changed my life". People have given me such wonderful feedback. When people say to you, "you have changed my life, I've got a life now, I can now go forward", it almost feels as if they are talking about somebody else. It's a wonderful thing to hear, but I know that they are not just talking about me but also those in the Spirit world who have come in to be with us.

I feel humbled when I think back over what I have seen.

When you see someone come in for a reading and their face is down, they are hardly talking to you, and they are so sad because of whom they have recently lost, and then you see them go out the front door with a big smile on their face and they give you a huge hug or a kiss on the cheek, that is the humbling bit. It is that knowing that I have made a difference.

A Lifetime Of Learning

I have learned so much from others on my journey. When my pathway led me to mediumship and self-development I was blessed with a number of good teachers and mediums each teaching me from their own experience, and yet advising me to be myself and find my own way of doing things; to find my own standards but to never stop searching for excellence. "In search of excellence" are my watchwords, my motto, and I know they always will be.

I like to watch other mediums work, I can tell a lot about the person from the demonstration they are giving. I look for the passion in the work they do, I like to see them link closely with the recipient of the messages, and of course I like to see the reaction to the information that has been given. I have talked to many excellent mediums, who have guided me just by chatting about their work and experiences, and sharing with me the dedication they have in connecting people with their loved ones and friends in the world of Spirit.

My whole life has been one of learning, both learning to accept who I am and learning to deal with the difficulties and losses that we all suffer from time to time. You might think that because mediums are in touch with the Spirit world that they live a charmed life. But that is certainly not the case. A lot of mediums that I know have had to pull themselves up by the bootstraps, and some of them are still struggling. Like them I have had my own trials and tribulations including times of doubt, difficulty and disappointment. At the same time I can see that in some ways I have been blessed. I can also see that the difficulties and losses that I have experienced have helped me to understand and empathise when people come to me in their own dark times.

Being a medium brings its own challenges as you will probably have realised by now. There will be peaks and troughs in your experience. And you will never stop learning. So if you have just started out with your development, in the words of the Boy Scouts movement, "be prepared." Also, be aware that a three week course does not make you a medium. You need to work at being a medium and be able to make a thorough connection with people from the world of Spirit so that you can give details about the person you have connected with. It is in the details that you will convince your recipient and yourself that your connection is real and accurate. You can't learn that in weeks, it takes years, decades even.

Choose your teachers carefully and wisely. Even if they or their institute have a big name that doesn't necessarily mean that they are the right teachers for you. Once you get under way you will witness a rollercoaster of emotions, not only your own but those of the families and friends of the many people you will be drawn to help. You will be experiencing the emotions of those who are coming through and of those who are receiving the messages. You will notice that your senses will come more and more to the surface, not only your psychic senses but many of your inner senses as well. I discovered that the more I learned and demonstrated my mediumship the more I became aligned with my inner self which is something that at times was not an easy connection to make.

Eventually I acknowledged that the senses are like a tool

in my psychic toolbox, and that learning to control how I handled them was beneficial for myself in many ways. I was accepting who I really was as a medium. I found out that I could absorb and pass on emotions from the world of Spirit. Those emotions helped me to emphasise or make messages clearer to my recipient. This meant that they could feel the message, feel the personalities of their friends and relatives, so that if only for a few minutes they could be in the company of those they loved once again.

As I have mentioned in several chapters in this book sometimes the emotional part of my work tested me very hard, and there were times when I swore that I would give up this work as a medium, as a connector. Yet every time I have had those thoughts some person has called me on the phone in floods of tears grieving from the loss of a loved one and needing counselling or mediumship. Whenever I have recommended another medium instead, the person who has contacted me is insistent that it must be me they want to talk to. They have either seen me work from the rostrum, or a friend or relative has visited me for an appointment and given me the thumbs up. Some have been pointed in my direction from other mediums, which is a real accolade.

I can even remember my sister Carol arriving at my front door arm in arm with a friend who was in tears, asking if I would help her friend, who was going through so many difficulties in life followed more recently by the death of her father. I found the strength to say that I had decided to give up this work, but it didn't help when the poor soul dried her eyes and blew her nose on her handkerchief saying that she understood, and she was sorry for disturbing me. Well I felt so bad, I felt that somebody had smacked me around the ear with a wet fish. I had so many emotions all at once, I think my first thoughts were 'How on earth can you let this person just walk away,' I felt guilty down to my socks, feeling I was letting my sister down, myself down and also the poor soul that I was turning away.

Of course I had to call her back and at least have a preliminary chat, then arrange an appointment at my earliest opportunity. Obviously once we had linked with the world of Spirit and passed on the necessary information from her loved ones and family she began to feel better and visited me again at a happier time.

More Surprises

When I think back at how many people have been introduced to me or introduced themselves to me in unusual ways it does make me laugh. Here is one story that I have to share with you.

I remember a lady ringing me from her home in America. She was withholding her number so I very nearly didn't answer the call. (too many scam and spam calls.)

I answered the phone and a strong southern American accent came over the speakerphone.

"Is that Rod Mackay" she bellowed

"*Roy* Mackay" I replied.

"What's in a name"? she retorted

"It helps me acknowledge when somebody is talking to me" I replied

"Oh wise guy" she returned.

I was finding it hard to hold back my laughter.

"You talk to the dead I hear, is that you"?

"I am a medium madam, if that helps".

"It doesn't", came the reply

"Can I help you or have you called long distance to insult me" I said, at this stage the conversation was becoming tedious.

"So" she continued, "if you can talk to the dead I may

wish to make an appointment with you." I gave her my website address but she just talked over me. I explained that if she would glance at my website she might be able to ascertain if I was the person she was looking for regarding a reading.

"If you are genuine," she mumbled "then I would like you to answer three complimentary questions for me.

"Madam" I replied, "first of all it is 11p.m. here and you have interrupted my evening or should I say night."

She interrupted me again, "Well it's only afternoon here." "Do I get three complimentary questions then"?

"I am sorry madam", I continued, "I do not just switch on whenever somebody wants me to, there is a procedure I have to go through to achieve a link".

By now I was exasperated and I said: "Madam, I am willing to help whenever I can if you wish to make an appointment at a more acceptable time". I heard her grunt for want of a better word.

Then I added and I really do not know where this remark came from and I do regret it: "Does your psychiatrist give three complimentary sessions"?

Truly, I wanted to say dentist, but it just didn't come out that way. And I am hoping that as she put the phone down on me she may not have heard the word psychiatrist. I am only human after all, though I feel bad now even sharing this with you.

There have been other surprises too. One of the funniest was when I was giving a reading at home and one of my best mates from school, who died some time ago, walked into the room where I was with my sitter and said, "Watcha mate, so is this how it works, then?"

I had to say to him in my mind, "Not now, I am busy". He laughed and left soon afterwards. That was irritating but lovely. I have also seen my mum and nan, and I know it was them, it was not a dream.

Some surprises have been awkward. There was one occasion when I was giving a reading to a lady, and I was being shown from the world of Spirit some really lovely underwear. I was thinking, 'Oh my goodness what have I got here,' because sometimes negative entities can come in and try to disrupt a reading. I wasn't sure what to say, so I said to the lady:

"I am picking up something and I'm not sure how to say it".

She said, "Go on".

I replied, "It's a bit embarrassing. I am seeing this lady just showing me underwear".

My sitter then said, "Oh really, what sort of underwear."

I thought 'this lady is having fun with me because she knows it's embarrassing.

She added, "What colour are you seeing?"

"Pink", I said.

Then she went further asking me, "Has she got a dress on?"

"No",

It turned out that my sitter had started her own business creating lingerie, it was her grandmother who was connecting with her.

The other awkward surprise that sticks in my mind was when I was in Canada and giving a public presentation to a hall full of people, and I was interrupted by a lady in the Spirit world. I've mentioned this in an earlier chapter. This insistent lady, who kept saying, "I want to talk to my daughter," was startling and disconcerting because I was already in communication with another spirit. At first I didn't know what to do, so I thought the only thing I can do is to speak out aloud to the audience, so they could see what was happening. Luckily they could see the funny side, and they all got a great laugh out of it.

Face To Face With The Past

In my work as a medium I have sometimes been taken a long way back into the past. I have occasionally seen people from centuries ago wearing very different clothes from today. The most unusual appearance I have seen was a Knight Templar. I have seen two or three of those in my time, and in each case they have been standing next to the person sitting in front of me. They are standing there as a guide for them. They come in wearing heavy chain mail with the great cross, and the white tabard. They always appear in the same way, standing with their hands resting on their sword.

I have also seen a highwayman. A gentleman came to see me for a reading, and the spirits who connected with me were talking about somebody around him, who was not to be trusted and then suddenly I saw a person with a mask over his face and a three cornered hat, wearing a big black cloak and holding a pistol. He looked like the highwayman Dick Turpin. The gentlemen in front of me understood completely, and said, "Yes he would rob his own grandmother".

I once saw Florence Nightingale, and I felt that she was actually linked with the lady having the reading. Much of the reading revealed the various illnesses of members of her family including herself. So it seemed clear to me that Florence Nightingale was keeping an eye on the family and supporting the lady through a difficult time.

Bringing People Together

Although as I've said being a medium has tested me quite a lot, so much so that at times I didn't want to continue, it has also brought me great enjoyment. Seeing people in the saddest of places when I meet them and then going out with the biggest smiles, that is wonderful. I have also loved working in churches. There has been many a time when a church's committee member has had to run across the pews with a box of tissues for a lady or gentleman, because they have suddenly had warm words from a relative or friend in Spirit. When you see that you know that something special has happened.

When you work in a church you see so many different emotions. Sometimes you find that the person in Spirit and their recipient in the congregation are arguing just like they used to do when they were together. One of them will say, "you shouldn't have done it that way, I told you not to," and then the person in the congregation comes back and retaliates. People listening in the church will watch amazed. I love that, I guess I'm a bit of a showman. And then of course you get the odd one who doesn't want to have the connection that you make, like the woman who didn't want to hear from her departed husband. She wanted to be connected to someone else, but it doesn't work like that. We can't compel Spirit people to come. They come if they want to.

So it has been a fascinating and rewarding time. The more I think about these things the more I can see how lucky I have been with the experiences I have had. To have been able to help people in the way that I have, with the help of my guides and the spirits who have come in, is something that I will always remember.

And finally, remember that you too can connect with

your loved ones who are in the world of Spirit. It just takes time and patience. At first you may only get a fleeting impression, but if you persist your connections will get stronger. And you will surprise yourself – and your loved ones too!

Thank you for staying the course with me and reaching the last page. I hope what you have read has assured you that there *is* a world beyond this one, and I hope that it will inspire you to make your own connections with the world of Spirit and in your own way. God bless you.

About Roy Mackay

Roy Mackay

Roy Mackay is an acclaimed medium with more than 45 years experience. He has worked in Britain and Canada and on the internet internationally via Skype, and in total has given hundreds of public demonstrations and private readings. He has received more than 100 reviews with a five star rating on www.freeindex.co.uk.

In addition, he has on many occasions come to the aid of a homeowner whose property has been disturbed by spirits and then helped those spirits to move fully into the next world, so that the homeowner and their family could live in a more peaceful and happier environment. He has sometimes taken on this role when no one else would help.

Roy is trained in Reiki and is a certified Master Reiki Practitioner. He is also a speaker and teacher on the subject of mediumship, healing, meditation etc.

He is also a minister, authorised to officiate at weddings, baptisms and funerals.

Roy's website is: www.roymackay.co.uk
email: RFM236@ntlworld.com

Printed in the United States
By Bookmasters